Portraits of Jesus

Portraits of Jesus

A Reading Guide

Fourth Edition

Robert Imperato

HAMILTON BOOKS
AN IMPRINT OF
ROWMAN & LITTLEFIELD
Lanham • Boulder • New York • London

Published by Hamilton Books
An imprint of The Rowman & Littlefield Publishing Group, Inc.
4501 Forbes Boulevard, Suite 200, Lanham, Maryland 20706
www.rowman.com

86-90 Paul Street, London EC2A 4NE, United Kingdom

British Library Cataloguing in Publication Information Available

Library of Congress Cataloging-in-Publication Data Available

Names: Imperato, Robert, 1945– author.
Title: Portraits of Jesus: a reading guide / Robert Imperato.
Description: Fourth edition. | Lanham, MD: Hamilton Books, an imprint of Rowman
  & Littlefield, [2022] | Includes bibliographical references and index. | Summary:
  "This is an introductory guide to the ways Jesus is depicted in the New Testament.
  Attention to Jesus' political and historical contexts help to clarify the one Jesus behind
  the diverse portrayals"—Provided by publisher.
Identifiers: LCCN 2022025516 (print) | LCCN 2022025517 (ebook)
  | ISBN 9780761873341 (paperback) | ISBN 9780761873358 (epub)
Subjects: LCSH: Jesus Christ—Person and offices—Biblical teaching. | Bible.
  Gospels—Criticism, interpretation, etc.
Classification: LCC BT203 .I47 2022 (print) | LCC BT203 (ebook) | DDC 232/.8—dc23/
  eng/20220718
LC record available at https://lccn.loc.gov/2022025516
LC ebook record available at https://lccn.loc.gov/2022025517

Contents

Acknowledgments

I am grateful for Ellie Rose Sanchez, Ethan Paolo Sanchez, and Robyn Elliott Panares Tuban.

Introduction

This reading guide intends to assist students with an introductory reading of the New Testament. The first chapter offers a historically plausible understanding of Jesus that is rooted in all four gospels. Although far from comprehensive this can serve as an historical background to the later chapters. The subsequent chapters focus on the ways individual evangelists adapted their understanding to their particular audiences and to their own agendas.

Unlike the early readers of the New Testament, contemporary students may benefit from many centuries of reflection. In modern times when the four gospels were read in parallel columns, readers could see the adjustments made by different evangelists. One may often explain these adjustments in terms of different audiences, writing styles, and editorial emphases arising from differing values. A popular, though inadequate attempt to explain differences between Gospels is along the lines of four different people remembering the same event differently. As we move through this text, I believe the weakness of that understanding will become obvious. We will be following the broadly accepted and well-founded assumption of the chronological priority of Mark's Gospel. To see how the authors of Matthew's and Luke's Gospel make small changes to Mark is easy to track, and we will not assume that Matthew, Mark, or Luke were eyewitness reporters. (For the sake of brevity Mark, Matthew, Luke, and John will refer to the Gospels that bear those names.) The nature of these Gospels is not news reporting, rather the material is shaped by the authors to affect their readers' understanding of Christian life and of Jesus, the central inspiration of their discipleship.

The contributions of Paul and John will fill out this reading guide. Their insights have shaped Christian understanding as profoundly as anyone, even though Paul's encounter with Jesus was mystical rather than in the flesh, and it is uncertain how much access the author of John's Gospel had to the Gospels of Matthew, Mark, or Luke.

Sensitivity to how each author shapes the material in his work to highlight particular meanings may generate more questions than answers. The "portraits" approach however, is designed to give students more than questions. The intentions of authors are retrievable, and portraits offer a synthetic balance to the useful work of analysis.

Aside from literary analysis, this fourth edition offers more historical information than earlier versions. The New Testament is composed of historically conditioned documents. While this reading guide does not attempt to sort out comprehensively what is historical from what is not, nevertheless attention to historically grounded material is important if understandings of Jesus are to be more than functions of the imaginations of early followers. In this latest edition aside from the first chapter on Jesus as prophet, each portrait will be situated in relevant historical settings. A lengthy appendix gives some of the relevant details about the history of Israel. Knowledge of history is inescapable if the world in which Jesus and New Testament writers lived is to be comprehended.

Christians have over time removed study of Jesus from his original historical setting in order to make him relevant for all times. Placing him back in history may make some of his original issues less pertinent to a contemporary reader, such as how the Temple in Jerusalem ought to be run. The mismanagement of the Jerusalem Temple is remote from the interests of most, but that is the cost of historical knowledge. At the same time, Jesus' involvement in his political world may suggest the significance to his followers of engaging in the social issues of their day. Above this question is the more important one of inching ahead for a more accurate understanding. In reading the Gospels it is appropriate to raise the question about each text whether the story or parable or saying comes from the time of Jesus or from the time of the writing of the Gospel. For example, does the parable of the vineyard in Mark 12 include Jesus' comment on the attempt of vineyard workers to seize profit from the wealthy vineyard owner or is the parable commenting on the destruction of the Temple decades after Jesus? Going back and forth from the time of Jesus to the time of the Gospel writer will often disclose neglected insights.

This book is intended as a guide to the text of the New Testament; it would be best to continuously refer to the New Testament rather than read this in isolation. Before reading each chapter, I would recommend processing the questions listed at the beginning of each chapter, using primarily the New Testament as resource. Afterward the chapters may fill in some gaps.

Chapter 1

Jesus as Prophet

One Jesus or Many?

It is easy to sketch the various portraits of Jesus, and such a literary approach can help to sensitize the reader to the values and intentions of the different authors of the New Testament. This book is primarily designed to clarify those intentions and portraits. Much more challenging is to determine how these disparate views cohere around a single person.

Both theologians and historians in their search for the real Jesus have their own built in biases. For example, theologians in general would want theological conclusions about Jesus as Divine to endure, despite any signs of weakness or error associated with Jesus in the New Testament (e.g., Jesus baptized or Jesus referring to the wrong prophet concerning 30 pieces of silver, etc.). Some historians, on the other hand, would be skeptical about the miraculous.

What can serve as a check against reducing Jesus into a projection of human need, a projection of what people want to find in Jesus? Consider Carl Jung's description of the psychological experience of reading the New Testament where Jesus represents and evokes the ideal image of the reader's ideal self. As Jesus broke with conventional living to pursue the call of God, so too the reader is thereby encouraged to break with convention to follow the call of God. (See his *The Development of Personality*, 167+.) This is true, but this process is identical to what happens to a Buddhist reading about Gautama, but Jesus and Gautama are not identical. What is to protect Christianity from a purely generic God or hero? History can serve to challenge human projection. Who was Jesus in his historical reality?

Since Jesus lived in history, historical analysis may add to the understanding of Jesus. Historians have built in limitations namely to restrict inquiry to what occurs in space and time and to past events that are somewhat similar to present events. What historians can affirm about Jesus may ignore what Christians value most about Jesus, for example his resurrection and ascension which are radically different from contemporary events and go beyond space

1

and time. As a result of the limitations of historical inquiry, theologians can either ignore history in favor of faith or more realistically locate historical inquiry to a valuable but subordinate role to faith.

Historically minded scholars have come up with various criteria to sort out the historical from the theological. This is a nearly impossible task, though it is a respectable attempt to take history seriously. Such criteria include the criterion of embarrassment when there are statements or events that go against what early Christian writers would have wanted (e.g., Jesus in a subordinate relationship to John the Baptist in the baptism of Jesus). Anything in the New Testament that early Christians would not have wanted to invent would most likely be historically grounded. Was Jesus baptized or not? One could argue this would have been so embarrassing to early Christianity that the early Christians would never have invented a scene where Jesus was subordinate to John the Baptist. In addition, the incongruity of a sinless Jesus participating in a baptism of repentance would not likely have been welcomed by an early Christian publicist. On the other hand, one could argue that it would benefit early Christianity to have Jesus associated with such a well-known and esteemed prophet as John the Baptist, who was called a "good man" by Josephus, a Jewish historian contemporaneous to the New Testament (*Antiquities*, 18.5.2). Competing interpretations of the historicity of the baptism of Jesus yields appropriate uncertainty. (See Rodriguez, R., "The Embarrassing Truth about Jesus.")

Multiple attestation is another criterion that has some credibility. If more than one source attests to something and they are not copying from each other, that would give historical weight to the sayings or events. There are other criteria, but these are most useful. The problem with them is they can easily reinforce the biases of the person applying them. It is all too easy to discover what one wants to discover and to reinforce one's assumptions along the way.

To resist confirmation bias, Dale Allison describes "recurrent attestation." Instead of focusing on a single statement or event one would do better to attend to ideas and events which occur in many places in the New Testament. "The early Jesus tradition is not a collection of totally disparate and wholly unrelated materials. On the contrary, certain themes and motifs and rhetorical strategies are consistently attested over a wide range of material" (Allison, Dale, "How to Marginalize the Traditional Criteria of Authenticity," in Porter, Stanley E., and Tom Holmén, *Handbook for the Study of the Historical Jesus*, Brill, 2011, 24–25). This understanding presupposes that the followers of Jesus grasped the general messages of Jesus.

Jesus was an itinerant teacher so he could repeat his message often to ever changing audiences. Those followers who accompanied him from place to place would likely hear the same parables and stories again and again. Jesus would be an exceptionally poor teacher if those disciples totally missed his message. Human memory is better at grasping the gist of what happened or of what was said rather than small details. I have a friend who worked in a bank where there was a robbery. Thirty minutes after the robbery, one teller reported the robber wore a red hat; another teller said there was no hat. Details were lost, but they all agreed there was a robbery. The gist or general impression was obtained despite the disparity over details. Jesus' traditions vary over details, but it is not unreasonable to assert that the followers of Jesus grasped the general messages of Jesus. (See Allison, *Constructing Jesus*; Baker, 2010, chapter one on human memory.)

Rather than trying to separate the historical from non-historical, it is sounder and more productive to recreate as much of the historical contexts of Jesus and of the New Testament writers as possible. The work of Richard Horsley is especially helpful in this matter.

How would Jesus have been understood by his contemporaries? What broad descriptor would have attached to him which also would fit this criterion of recurrent attestation and thus would be rooted in history? In the Gospels of Matthew, Mark, and Luke, Jesus asks who people think he is, and the response was: is "John the Baptist; and others say, Elijah; and others one of the prophets" (Mark 8:28; Luke 9:19). Matthew adds "Jeremiah" to this list of prophets (Mt 16:13). Even in John's Gospel, people acknowledge him as a prophet: "This is indeed the prophet who is to come into the world!" (John 6:14; see also 4:19). He also refers to himself as speaking for God, a prophetic role: "My teaching is not mine, but his who sent me" (John 7:16). Some of the same tensions are present in both John's Gospel and the Synoptics (meaning the Gospels of Matthew, Mark and Luke), namely Jesus criticizes how the Temple is managed (John 2:13–22; Mk 11; Mt 21; Lk 19) and is criticized for healing on the Sabbath (John 5:16; Mk 3; Mt 12; Lk 13). Why did people think of him as a prophet? In part because he challenged the way society was being run both in Jerusalem and in Galilee (Mark 12 and parallels in Matthew 23). Biblical prophets were not so much future predictors as people who challenged people, especially those in power to conform to God's will.

Jesus spoke like a prophet and condemned similar actions to those condemned by Hebrew prophets. A few citations will make the point.

Biblical prophets condemn exploitation of the poor:

Therefore because you trample on the poor and take from them levies of grain, you have built houses of hewn stone, but you shall not live in them; you have planted pleasant vineyards, but you shall not drink their wine. (Amos 5:11)

Alas for those who are at ease in Zion, and for those who feel secure on Mount Samaria, the notables of the first of the nations, to whom the house of Israel resorts! (Amos 6:1)

The Lord enters into judgment with the elders and princes of his people: It is you who have devoured the vineyard; the spoil of the poor is in your houses. (Isaiah 3:14)

Woe to those who join house to house, who add field to field, until there is no more room, and you are made to dwell alone in the midst of the land. (Isaiah 5:8)

Woe to you, scribes and Pharisees, hypocrites! for you devour widows' houses and for a pretense you make long prayers. (Mt 23:14; Lk 20:47; Mk 12:40)

Prophets challenged dishonest religious and political leaders who engage unjust labor practices and money grubbing:

Hear this, you heads of the house of Jacob and rulers of the house of Israel, who abhor justice and pervert all equity, who build Zion with blood and Jerusalem with wrong. Its heads give judgment for a bribe, its priests teach for hire, its prophets divine for money; yet they lean upon the Lord and say, "Is not the Lord in the midst of us? No evil shall come upon us." (Micah 3:9–11)

Woe to him who builds his house by unrighteousness, and his upper rooms by injustice; who makes his neighbor serve him for nothing, and does not give him his wages; . . . you have eyes and heart only for your dishonest gain, for shedding innocent blood, and for practicing oppression and violence. (Jeremiah 22:13–17)

And he taught, and said to them, "Is it not written, 'My house shall be called a house of prayer for all the nations?' But you have made it a den of robbers." (Mk 11:17, also Jeremiah 11:17)

Biblical prophets call for justice:

Thus says the Lord: "Go down to the house of the king of Judah, and speak there this word, and say, 'Hear the word of the Lord, O King of Judah, who sit on the throne of David, you, and your servants, and your people who enter these gates. Thus says the Lord: Do justice and righteousness, and deliver from the hand of the oppressor him who has been robbed. And do no wrong or violence to the alien, the fatherless, and the widow, nor shed innocent blood in this place.'" (Jer 22:1–3)

Woe to you, scribes and Pharisees! for you tithe mint, dill, and cumin, and have neglected the weightier matters of the law: justice and mercy and faith. (Mt 23:23)

Prophets announce restoration:

Then I will gather the remnant of my flock out of all the countries where I have driven them, and I will bring them back to their fold, and they shall be fruitful and multiply. I will set shepherds over them who will care for them, and they shall fear no more, nor be dismayed, neither shall any be missing, says the LORD. (Jeremiah 23: 3–4)

But seek first his kingdom and his righteousness, and all these things will be given to you as well. (Mt 6:33)

There was given to him the book of the prophet Isaiah. He opened the book and found the place where it was written, "The Spirit of the Lord is upon me, because he has anointed me to preach good news to the poor. He has sent me to proclaim release to the captives and recovering of sight to the blind, to set at liberty those who are oppressed, to proclaim the acceptable year of the Lord." And he closed the book, and gave it back to the attendant, and sat down; and the eyes of all in the synagogue were fixed on him. And he began to say to them, "Today this scripture has been fulfilled in your hearing." (Lk 4:17–21)

Matthew 23 (with parallels in Luke 11) has Jesus in the style of Hebrew prophets railing against "scribes and Pharisees" over their burdening others, their hypocrisy, and their murdering prophets sent by God.

Woe to you, scribes and Pharisees, hypocrites! for you tithe mint and dill and cumin, and have neglected the weightier matters of the law, justice and mercy and faith; these you ought to have done, without neglecting the others. You blind guides, straining out a gnat and swallowing a camel! (Mt 23:23–24)

I send you prophets and wise men and scribes, some of whom you will kill and crucify, and some you will scourge in your synagogues and persecute from town to town. (Mt 23:34)

Jesus' utterances blend into the message and style of Hebrew prophets throughout Matthew, Mark, and Luke.

Jesus was literally (not figuratively) a martyr, that is, he witnessed to his understanding of God and people and was willing to put his life in jeopardy to promote his understanding of God, relationship with God, his understanding of how people ought to be treated, and how a corrupt administration was at odds with human dignity. People do not like to be told that they should change how to live. A common response to challenge is anger.

This kind of challenge has generated stories of prophets who are martyred, and Jesus is part of that tradition according to Luke: "Nevertheless I must go on my way today and tomorrow and the day following; for it cannot be that a prophet should perish away from Jerusalem" (13:33). 2 Chronicles 24:21 refers to stoning death of Jeremiah. The Jewish apocrypha work "Lives of the Prophets" says Isaiah was killed, as was Zechariah son of Jehoiada, and Amos.

Jewish martyrs are featured in 2 Maccabees when Greeks were forcing Jews to eat pork. Rather than disobey their beliefs by eating pork, some were fried to death. Giving good example is how the martyr's death benefits others. 2 Maccabees also invites others to die nobly:

> Eleazar, one of the scribes in high position, a man now advanced in age and of noble presence, was being forced to open his mouth to eat swine's flesh. But he, welcoming death with honor rather than life with pollution, went up to the rack of his own accord, spitting out the flesh, as men ought to go who have the courage to refuse things that it is not right to taste, even for the natural love of life. (2 Macc 6:18–20)

> . . . by manfully giving up my life now, I will show myself worthy of my old age and leave to the young a noble example of how to die a good death willingly and nobly for the revered and holy laws. (2 Macc 6:27–28)

4 Maccabees also emphasizes the example of the martyrs:

> For all people, even their torturers, marveled at their courage and endurance, and they became the cause of the downfall of tyranny over their nation. By their endurance they conquered the tyrant, and thus their native land was purified through them. (4 Macc 1:11)

The idea of good example carries over into the gospels. "Imitation" (or re-enactment) is not mentioned in Luke's Gospel, but it is implied: "Whoever does not carry his own cross and come after me cannot be my disciple" (14:27).

If one views Jesus' life and death as that of a martyr, his benefit to people comes about by others following, imitating, and re-enacting his teaching and his example, just as the example of the Jewish martyrs helped to liberate Israel from Greek rule.

JESUS' PROTEST

The corrupt administration that Jesus was protesting was Roman rule (Mk 5:9) supported by King Herod and his sons who tyrannically spied on people (Josephus, *Antiquities*, 15.10.4) and taxed the peasant population of Israel. In general, subsistent farmers had to give 25% of their crop yields every second year as "tribute" to Rome (Josephus, *Antiquities*, 14.10.5–6). As one Jewish resister said of Roman taxation: "this taxation was no better than an introduction to slavery, and exhorted the nation to assert their liberty" (Josephus, *Antiquities*, 18.1.1). Although money given to the Temple was supposed to support the Temple, Pilate found ways of using that money for other building projects and had protestors of this misuse of funds beaten (Josephus, *Jewish Wars*, 2.9.4).

The Jerusalem Temple, though managed by priests, was under Herodian and Roman control. For example, in the time of Jesus a Roman official appointed the High Priest: "Valerius Gratus [succeeded by Pontius Pilate] appointed Ismael, the son of Phabi, to be High Priest" (Josephus, *Antiquities*, 18.2.2). Money making in the Temple served the interests of the Temple state, the religious elite, the Herodians, and the Romans, at the expense of the peasant population. "He [Pilate] raised another disturbance, by expending that sacred treasure which is called Corban upon aqueducts, whereby he brought water from the distance of four hundred furlongs . . . " (Josephus, *Wars*, 2.9.4; also *Antiquities*, 18.3.2).

Jesus was interfering with the way the Temple was being run; this would have disturbed both the priests, the Herodians, and the Romans. Jesus' action in the Temple threatened the alliance between the Jerusalem priesthood and the Romans.

Jesus' protest against taxation was subtle: "Take the first fish that comes up, and when you open its mouth you will find a shekel; take that and give it to them for me and for yourself" (Mt 17:24–26). The comment about finding a shekel in a fish's mouth humorously suggests how unlikely money was going to come from the hands of Galilean peasants!

How does Jesus' protest in the Temple fit with the saying "Render to Caesar the things that are Caesar's, and to God the things that are God's" (Mk 12:17)? This saying might well have concealed Jesus' true feelings. Jesus was not trying to extract money from Galilee for the sake of the Temple state! "He is clearly dissembling in public about his everyday resistance agenda" (Oakman, *The Politics of Jesus*, 105).

For Jesus' hearers "the things that are God's" means everything, as everything belonged to God. Had he said, "Do not pay taxes," he likely would have been arrested. Instead, he says to the people, give to God what belongs to God. Fidelity to the covenant means not bowing down or paying tribute to any but God; there was no separation of church and state in the theocracy in which Jesus lived. Everything belonged to God; paying tribute to Caesar was not being faithful (see Horsley, *The Politics of Roman Palestine*, 51, 120–121). (Paul in Romans 13, unlike Jesus, was living outside of Israel, and thus primarily addressing Gentiles.)

Paying tribute or taxes to Rome would have been seen by some Judeans as violating the first commandment about other gods.

> And now Archelaus's part of Judea was reduced into a province, and Coponius, one of the equestrian order among the Romans, was sent as a procurator, having *the power of [life and] death* put into his hands by Caesar. Under his administration it was, that a certain Galilean, whose name was Judas, prevailed with his countrymen to revolt, and said they were cowards, if they would endure to pay a tax to the Romans, and would, after God, *submit to mortal men as their lords.* (Josephus, *Wars*, 2.8.1)

This quotation suggests severe punishment was possible for open tax resistance. (See also *Antiquities*, 18.1.6.)

Since many commentators imply a separation of Church and state when discussing Mark 12:17, a couple of touch points support the opinion that Jesus was not totally accepting of Roman taxation:

> But you say, "If a man tells his father or his mother, 'Whatever you would have gained from me is Corban' (that is, given to God)—then you no longer permit him to do anything for his father or mother, thus making void the word of God by your tradition that you have handed down." (Mk 7:11–13)

If Jesus opposes depriving parents of support in the name of Temple offering, how much more would this apply to Roman taxation?

Similarly Jesus' challenge to people lording over others would apply to Roman rulers and their surrogates:

> And Jesus called them to him and said to them, "You know that those who are considered rulers of the Gentiles lord it over them, and their great ones exercise authority over them. But it shall not be so among you. But whoever would be great among you must be your servant." (Mk 12:42–43)

A practical implication of this rule by Romans was taxation.

Jesus was known to have undivided loyalty to God; he would not be indifferent to the idolatrous association of tax payment to the Romans. "No one can serve two masters . . . " (Mt 6:24). "You shall love the Lord your God with all your heart and with all your soul and with all your mind and with all your strength." (Mk 12:30; see Gibson 312). Undivided loyalty to God would have been in tension with taxes imposed by Romans who had traditions of deifying their emperors.

Religion and politics were difficult, and in many cases impossible, to separate in Israel in the times of Jesus. The Herodians had the help of the religious elite who tried to control the behavior of its oppressed population (Mark 2 and 7). Jesus did his best to challenge the stranglehold this administration had over the people by pointing out how some of the rules of his day were too restrictive and missed the broader picture: "The Sabbath was made for man, not man for the Sabbath" (Mk 2). Those religious leaders had the protection of the governing authorities as long as they cooperated.

Jesus was understood to be similar to Hebrew prophets of old: he did miraculous healings like Elijah (1 Kgs 17 parallel with Luke 7:11+) while distancing himself from Elijah's use of violence (Lk 9:54–55). Jesus interpreted to the people the commandments associated with the prophet Moses (Mk 7; Mt 5:17+; Mt 15:4+). He also challenged the way the Temple was being run as did the prophet Jeremiah (Jer 7:11,15; Mk 11:17). He offered liberation not from Egyptian slavery but from oppression by the wealthy exploiting the poor (Mk 10:21–25; Lk 2:52; 6:20).

Outside of the Bible and near the times of Jesus and of the New Testament, Josephus (47–55 CE) notes a number of movements led by prophets to attempt to free people from Herodian and Roman rule. One prophet was Theudas:

> Now it came to pass, while Fadus was procurator of Judea, that a certain magician, whose name was Theudas, persuaded a great part of the people to take their effects with them, and follow him to the river Jordan. For he told them he was a prophet: and that he would, by his own command, divide the river, and afford them an easy passage over it. And many were deluded by his words. However, Fadus did not permit them to make any advantage of his wild attempt: but sent a troop of horsemen out against them. Who falling upon them unexpectedly, slew many of them, and took many of them alive. They also took Theudas alive, and cut off his head, and carried it to Jerusalem. This was what befell the Jews in the time of Cuspius Fadus's government. (Josephus, *Antiquities*, 20.5; also mentioned in Acts 15)

Josephus refers to another prophet who was from Egypt who unsuccessfully attempted to liberate oppressed Jews:

> There came out of Egypt, about this time, to Jerusalem, one that said he was a prophet; and advised the multitude of the common people to go along with him to the mount of olives, as it was called; which lay over against the city, and at the distance of five furlongs. He said further that he would shew them from hence how, at his command, the walls of Jerusalem would fall down: and he promised

them that he would procure them an entrance into the city through those walls, when they were fallen down. Now when Felix was informed of these things, he ordered his soldiers to take their weapons, and came against them with a great number of horsemen and footmen, from Jerusalem; and attacked the Egyptian, and the people that were with him. He also slew four hundred of them, and took two hundred alive. But the Egyptian himself escaped out of the fight; but did not appear anymore. (Josephus, *Antiquities*, 20.8; thanks to Horsley, *Jesus and the Politics of Roman Palestine*, 39–40)

These liberation movements were inspired by the formation of the people of Israel under the earlier prophetic leadership of Moses and Joshua.

What does all of this about Jesus as prophet and as martyr prophet say about Jesus? How did he respond to Roman and Herodian oppression? While some responded with violence, Jesus did not go that far. Despite his likeness to the prophet Elijah, he distances himself from Elijah's history of violence (Lk 9:54–55). He was, however, confrontational with the religious elite and with those working in and managing the Temple. His overturning of the tables of the money changers triggered his arrest. The legal ground for killing Jesus would have been sedition. "The authors of sedition and tumult, or those who stir up the people, shall, according to their rank, either be crucified, thrown to wild beasts, or deported to an island" (*The Opinions of Julius Paulus*, 5.22.1; Oakman, *The Politics of Jesus*, 110–111). More positively despite Roman and Herodian subjugation, he promoted fidelity to God especially through the commandments (Mk 7:10; Mt 15), mercy (Lk 6:36), and cooperation with one another, including debt forgiveness (Mt 6:12).

JESUS' MISSION

Thanks to the Lord's Prayer, his local context of growing indebtedness and poverty helps to clarify Jesus' mission: give us daily bread and forgive debts (Mt 6; Lk 11). The prayer also hopes for God's rule: "your kingdom come," which is hardly the rule of the Romans or Herodians.

Aware of the poverty of the local population, Jesus tells his disciples to be content with whatever is offered: "Whenever you enter a town and they receive you, eat what is set before you" (Lk 10:8).

His message is to seek God's kingdom despite economic pressures and to spread God's rule on earth: "Therefore I tell you, do not be anxious about your life, what you shall eat, nor about your body, what you shall put on. For life is more than food, and the body more than clothing" (Lk 12:22–23).

His message is designed to give comfort to the oppressed; God will take care: "Blessed are you poor, for yours is the kingdom of God. Blessed are you that hunger now, for you shall be satisfied. Blessed are you that weep now, for you shall laugh" (Lk 6:20–21). "Thy kingdom come, . . . On earth as it is in heaven" (Mt 6:10).

The language that courses through Luke's Gospel of God putting down the mighty and raising up the lowly and putting down the rich and raising up the poor, reflects Jesus' mission within the context of economic oppression (Lk 1:52–52; 16:19–25; 19:8). Since the stress on the poor is largely in Luke's Gospel, it is difficult to establish how much the concern for the poor came from Jesus versus from Luke's agenda. Jesus, the son of a manual laborer, lived as a peasant in a society where most people were struggling to survive. "You will never get out till you have paid the last penny" (Mt 5:25). Poverty was part of Jesus' landscape. The petitions of the Lord's Prayer (Mt 6), feeding the hungry (Mk 6 and 8) the sermon on the plain ("Blessed are you poor" Lk 6), "when you give alms" (Mt 6), help to make the case that concern for the poor likely goes back to Jesus. In Mark's Gospel giving to the poor is intrinsic to following Jesus: "You lack one thing; go, sell what you have, and give to the poor" (10:21). He also highlights the precarious situation of those with riches. "How hard it will be for those who have riches to enter the kingdom of God!" (Mk 10:23). To ask if Jesus was concerned with the poor is close to asking if he was concerned with people.

HISTORICAL CONTEXT

To appreciate Jesus' world, it is useful to remember Jesus' historical context. The people living in Israel (also called Palestine) had been invaded and conquered by foreign powers for centuries, thanks in part to their location on a trade route between the Nile Valley and the Fertile Crescent. Roman invasion was violent and intolerable to many living in Israel.

Romans had a long history of violent conquest. The Roman historian Tacitus passes on description by a Caledonian enemy, Galacus, of Roman plundering style:

> Romans, from whose oppression escape is vainly sought by obedience and submission. Robbers of the world, having by their universal plunder exhausted the land, they rifle the deep. If the enemy be rich, they are rapacious; if he be poor, they lust for dominion; neither the east nor the west has been able to satisfy them. Alone among men they covet with equal eagerness poverty and riches. To robbery, slaughter, plunder, they give the lying name of empire; they make a solitude and call it peace. (*Agricola*, 30)

Josephus tells of the Romans enslaving 30,000 people in Galilee in their fight with Hasmoneans: "Cassius had fled into that province, and when he had taken possession of the same, he made a hasty march into Judea; and, upon his taking Taricheae, he carried thirty thousand Jews into slavery" (Josephus, *Jewish Wars*, 1.8.9). Taricheae is the Greek name for Magdala, Jesus' home turf. Though this enslavement happened maybe 80 or 90 years before Jesus, he and those in his region would have had memories of such trauma at the hands of the Romans (see Horsley, *Palestine*, 56+ for more details). In the time when Jesus lived, Josephus describes a protest against Pilate who had displayed images of Caesar in Jerusalem and outright rebellion against his raiding the sacred treasure for building an aqueduct (Josephus, *Antiquities*, 18.3.1–2; *Wars*, 2.9.3–4).

With the Roman conquest led by General Pompey the people in what the Romans called Judea (including both Galilee and Judah) were subject to taxation by the Romans but also by the puppet government headed by the King of the Jews, Herod. These economic burdens upon subsistence farmers led to increasing indebtedness and to some having to give up their land to become tenant farmers. Religious elites (scribes, Pharisees, Sadducees) kept the Herodian rule in power and served as surrogates to keep the people in line (Mk 7:1–9).

In addition to economic pressures, some religious nationalists (including "Zealots") were outraged at having to be ruled by the Romans and their appointed King and after his death, by his sons instead of their God. Josephus notes, "These men agree in all other things with the Pharisaic notions; but they have an inviolable attachment to liberty, and say that God is to be their only Ruler and Lord" (Josephus, *Antiquities*, 1.6). It is not surprising that the economic and social injustices and religious offenses generated a number of uprisings and protests. Jesus' entrance to Jerusalem and the Jerusalem Temple can rightly be seen to fit this historical pattern.

MESSIAH?

Jesus would likely have been understood in his time as a prophet, while many understood him to be messiah. The crowds hailing him as messiah at his entrance to Jerusalem demonstrates messianic hope among the local population. Their hope was fed by his powerful ministry (Mk 8:30) and O.T. prophecies, as well as more recent history. After the death of King Herod, there were uprisings associated with a messiah (Josephus, *Wars*, 2.4.2–3). The Dead Sea Scrolls hope for a messianic king who would "bring good news to the poor" (4Q521 "Messianic Apocalypse" of the Dead Sea Scrolls). Messianic hope endured long after Jesus (2 Baruch 72; 4 Ezra 12 and Bar Kochba). There are, however, reasons to put "messiah" slightly in the background. Messiah in the time of Roman occupation implied, among other things, military might. The messiah was expected to "purge Jerusalem from nations that trample (her) down to destruction" (*Psalms of Solomon*, 17). Jesus did not correspond to that expectation. Mark 8:31–33 has an argument between Peter and Jesus over the expectation that Jesus would take over the nation. He did not attempt to topple the government, and he would not likely have been entirely comfortable with that kind of militantly political role.

RELEVANCE

Although the issue of how to run the Jerusalem Temple has long ago ceased to be relevant to Christians, Jesus in his prophetic stance offers people potential inspiration to follow his example by speaking truth to power, and by reaching out to those who have been excluded, the hungry, the alien (Mt 25), the infirm, the people burdened by economic and political exploitation, and by encouraging forgiveness and mercy (Mt 5; Lk 6).

This chapter on Jesus as prophet is not intended to suggest that is all that Jesus was, but it is designed as a background perspective that is historically grounded; it furthermore offers a fairly unified understanding of Jesus which undergirds the particular emphases and agendas of individual New Testament writers found in the following chapters.

Chapter 2

Mark's Portrait of Jesus

God's Agent against Evil and Corruption, Hidden and Suffering Son of God

Key questions to pose of the text of Mark's Gospel:

1. Who are Jesus' enemies in Mark's Gospel and why were they opposed to Jesus?
2. Who are those who acknowledge Jesus as son of God?.
3. Who do not acknowledge Jesus as son of God?
4. What is Jesus' teaching on discipleship (ch. 8–10)?
5. How are the disciples characterized?
6. Why are they characterized in that way?
7. How does the pattern of recognition and lack of recognition relate to the teaching on discipleship (in ch. 8–10, 15:39)?

Discussion questions:

1. What specific language in Mark's Gospel is in opposition to the Romans?
2. Why was there antagonism between Jesus and the religious elite in ch. 2?
3. Why did the religious elite interpret the parable of the vineyard (Mk 12) as against them?

Mark's Gospel presents Jesus surrounded by opposition from a corrupt administration. This Temple state ultimately was under Roman rule but operated through a puppet government headed by Herod, and after his death, by his sons. Religious elites who wanted to keep their Temple and religious rules cooperated with this theocracy.

Mark's Gospel, written decades after Jesus, addresses people who face persecution (see Mark 4:17; 8:35, and 13:9+), beginning in 64 CE under Nero. It is likely part of Mark's audience feared Roman persecution and may have been traumatized by the Roman destruction of the Temple. Jesus is presented as an example of someone who did not run away from danger but who continued his mission.

PERSECUTION

Mark's Gospel suggests early Christians experienced persecution from Romans:

> But take heed to yourselves; for they will deliver you up to councils; and you will be beaten in synagogues; and you will stand before governors and kings for my sake, to bear testimony before them. And the gospel must first be preached to all nations. And when they bring you to trial and deliver you up, do not be anxious beforehand what you are to say; but say whatever is given you in that hour, for it is not you who speak, but the Holy Spirit. And brother will deliver up brother to death, and the father his child, and children will rise against parents and have them put to death; and you will be hated by all for my name's sake. But he who endures to the end will be saved. (Mark 13:9–12)

Although Christianity attempted to live harmoniously with the Romans, Christians did have difficulty with the Roman practice of honoring effigies of Roman emperors. This made them appear to be less than loyal inhabitants of Roman lands. Roman suspicion of Christians climaxed with Roman persecution. Romans worshipped a variety of gods, and this worship was associated with their ethnicity so Romans worshipped Roman gods. Christianity was exclusive in worshipping only one God with Jesus as son of God. Romans sometimes called Christians "atheists" because Christians did not worship their gods. "So after this all the multitude, marveling at the bravery of the God-beloved and God-fearing people of the Christians, raised a cry, 'Away with the atheists; let search be made for Polycarp'" (*Martyrdom of Polycarp*, 3:2; c.155–160 CE).

Jewish resistance and rebellions against the Romans contributed to Roman persecution of Jews. This persecution culminated in the destruction of the Temple in Jerusalem. Christians in Jerusalem honored and prayed in the Temple even after Jesus' death (Acts 2:46; 3:1). Borderlines between Christians and Jews were not sharply drawn. Christians at times would have been seen as part of the Jewish population (see Acts 18:2, 26). Both Christians (Tacitus, *Annals*, 15) and Jews (reported by Cicero in "Pro Flaccus," 28) were described as practicing "superstition" by Romans. Tacitus (c. 56-c. 120 CE) describes Christians (*Annals*, 15) and elsewhere Jews (*Histories*, 5) as hating humankind (more on this in the Luke chapter).

Capitalizing on the tensions between Romans and Christians, Nero blamed a fire in Rome on the vulnerable minority known as Christians:

> Nero fastened the guilt and inflicted the most exquisite tortures on a class hated for their abominations, called Christians by the populace. Christus, from whom the name had its origin, suffered the extreme penalty during the reign of Tiberius at the hands of one of our procurators, Pontius Pilatus, and a most mischievous superstition, thus checked for the moment, again broke out not only in Judaea, the first source of the evil, but even in Rome, where all things hideous and shameful from every part of the world find their centre and become popular. Accordingly, an arrest was first made of all who pleaded guilty; then, upon their information, an immense multitude was convicted, not so much of the crime of firing the city, as of hatred against mankind. Mockery of every sort was added to their deaths. Covered with the skins of beasts, they were torn by dogs and perished, or were nailed to crosses, or were doomed to the flames and burnt, to serve as a nightly illumination, when daylight had expired. (Tacitus, *Annals*, 15)

These sources of persecution of Christians and their consequent suffering may have found expression in Mark's presentation of Jesus' desolation and desperation on the cross: "Why have you forsaken me?" Christians and Jews were feeling abandoned by God, and some would have resonated with Jesus' desperate cry.

As the Temple was being attacked (c. 70 CE) there were Jews who believed a Jewish ruler (a messianic figure) would come to rescue them. The Roman historian Tacitus describes Jewish belief in the face of Roman assault: "Most people held the belief that, according to the ancient priestly writings, this was the moment at which the East was fated to prevail: they would now start forth from Judaea and conquer the world. This enigmatic prophecy really applied to Vespasian and Titus. But men are blinded by their hopes. The Jews took to themselves the promised destiny, and even defeat could not convince them of the truth" (*Histories*, 5.13). Jewish faith is likely to have been bolstered by biblical hope: "I see him, but not now; I behold him, but not near. A star shall come out of Jacob and a scepter will rise out of Israel. It shall crush the foreheads of Moab and break down all the sons of Seth. Edom shall be dispossessed" (Numbers 24:17–19). Josephus, rejected this thinking by rebellious Jews, "what did the most [to] elevate them in undertaking this war, was an ambiguous oracle that was also found in their sacred writings, how, 'about that time, one from their country should become governor of the habitable earth.' The Jews took this prediction to belong to themselves in particular, and many of the wise men were thereby deceived in their determination. Now this oracle certainly denoted the government of Vespasian, who was appointed emperor in Judea" (Josephus, *Jewish Wars*, 6.5.4). From this comment by Josephus, it is apparent that not all Jews engaged in messianic hope associated with Roman oppression.

While certain Jews expected the coming of a messiah to rescue them, Christians expected a second coming of their messiah. "And then they will see the Son of man coming in clouds with great power and glory" (Mk 13:26). Not all of those attracted to Jesus' preaching would have anticipated persecution; eventually they had to deal with it. When a 20th century Christian such as Martin Luther King Jr. could readily expect persecution to meet him in his quest for justice, earliest Christians on the other hand needed to be comforted and strengthened by the teaching given in Mark's Gospel. (See Mark 4:16,17 and 13:9+ on how to face persecution; 8:35 on losing life to persecution.) Furthermore, an element of secrecy would have served to keep Christians off of Roman radar: "To you has been given the secret of the Kingdom of God, but for those outside, everything comes in parables in order that, while seeing, they may see, but not perceive" (4:11–12).

An interpretive context for early Christians (generally called "apocalyptic") would have been to understand that suffering (tribulation) precedes vindication (restoration or resurrection): "you will be hated by all for my name's sake. But he who endures to the end will be saved" (Mk 13:13). (See Allison, Dale, *Constructing Jesus*, for numerous Jewish texts consonant with this pattern, e.g., Amos 9 after destruction comes restoration. Also, Baruch prays for an end to death after suffering in *Syriac Baruch*, 21.) It would be easy in this context for many early Christians to expect their resurrection after their suffering.

Though both Christians and Jews experienced Roman persecution, most Roman persecution came after Jesus. There were instances of Jewish persecution of Christians: Acts of the Apostles (chapter 7) chronicles the persecution of Stephen. Paul himself refers to persecution repeatedly in 2 Corinthians (2 Corinthians 4:9,12:10, etc.), and Luke has Paul appealing to his Roman citizenship for protection (Acts 25:11). The Jewish persecution of Christianity comes from Christian teaching on Jesus as Divine and from Christian challenges to kosher dietary law and circumcision. There is, however, no recorded instance of judicial execution of a Christian by Jewish authorities. If it happened, and many question the historicity of the stoning of Stephen story (see Matthews, S., *Perfect Martyr*, 2012), it is likely to have been a type of mob killing (Hare, D., *The Theme of Jewish Persecution of Christians in St. Matthew*, 20).

Although Mark's Gospel aimed to support Christians who were oppressed and persecuted by Romans and to a far lesser degree by some Jews, there were older sources of hostility. What engaged Jesus of Nazareth is the oppression of Galileans and Judeans by religious elites who were cooperating with the Herodian regime who in turn were supported by the Romans. This takes us into reflection upon Jesus' mission which is distinguishable from the mission of Mark's Gospel. Occasionally this book will consider the mission of Mark's Gospel and alternately the mission of Jesus. (The parable of the vineyard from Mark 12 here illustrates these varying perspectives.)

JESUS' MISSION

Jesus' mission can be summarized in terms of two themes. One, calling people back to God, which included establishing God's kingdom or rule (Mk 1:14) and what Horsley calls "covenant renewal." And two, confrontation with harmful powers both cosmic and political. These themes are multiply attested in the Synoptic Gospels (e.g., Mt 5; Lk 6) and will surface in later chapters.

1. In Mark 1:14, after announcing the kingdom of God is at hand, Jesus begins to confront debilitating forces (1:23 ff.). In Mark 7, Jesus appeals to the Mosaic covenant in his argument with scribes and Pharisees:

> You leave the commandment of God, and hold fast the tradition of men. . . . You have a fine way of rejecting the commandment of God, in order to keep your tradition! (Mk 7:8–9)

This appeal assumes respect of the Mosaic covenant by Jesus' hearers. In that same chapter, Jesus argues with scribes and Pharisees and challenges their interpretation of Law and life that in this case undermines economic support for families:

> But you say, "If a man tells his father or his mother, 'What you would have gained from me is Corban' (that is, given to God) then you no longer permit him to do anything for his father or mother." (Mk 7:11–12)

The Mosaic covenant (Ex 20; Dt 5) involves the expectation of obedience by the Hebrew people who have been rescued from Egyptian slavery. That obedience includes loyalty to God rather than a human king (Judges 8:22–23) and not bowing down to images of others with the implication of giving them tribute: "You shall not bow down to them or serve them" (Dt 5:9). The other commandments are to maintain families (prohibition against adultery) which has obvious economic repercussions. Not to covet the goods of others: "Families might need protection against other villagers who might scheme to (covet) gain control of their resources (e.g., animals, produce) by theft, fraud, or false promises" (Horsley, *Politics of Roman Palestine*, 117).

2. Loyalty to God implies confrontation with toxic forces. In the Gospels, especially Mark's Gospel, there are numerous stories of demon possession and illnesses, all of which are pernicious: exorcism (1:25), the healing of Peter's mother-in-law (1:31), healings and exorcisms (1:35), healing of leper (1:41), challenge to the scribes (ch. 2 and early ch. 3), healing of paralytic (2:11), healing of man with withered hand (3:5), unclean spirits (3:11), Jesus accused of demon possession (3:22), exorcism of Legion (5:13), healing of woman with flow of blood (5:34), healing a little girl (5:42), healing people (6:5), making many well (6:56), healing/exorcism of daughter of Syrophoenician woman (7:29), healing of deaf man (7:35), healing of blind man (8:25), casting out deaf and dumb spirit (9:26), healing of blind man (10:53). All of these stories support the understanding of Jesus as God's agent in a battle against harmful forces: scribes, priests, Pharisees, Herodians (3:6), demons, bodily dysfunctions, and Romans (naming the unclean spirits with a Roman military term "Legion" in Mark 5 takes a subversive swipe at Roman occupation), which have crippled the people of Israel. Jesus is trying to establish God's kingdom, and the many healings and exorcisms show his alignment with God and his ability to bring evil powers into submission.

The rest of the Gospel (ch. 11+) demonstrates his willingness to confront the ruling powers in Jerusalem, who in turn kill him. The demon possession and illnesses are not separate from the corrupt administration in Jerusalem. The administration has the people in a state of degeneration of which the demons and illnesses are manifestations. Jesus is bringing "freedom" from the power of demons, from the restrictions of the scribes (hostility stories ch. 2, 3), as well as from the Romans (ch. 5). Those in positions of power enjoyed their wealth which Jesus also challenged: "How hard it will be for those who have riches to enter the kingdom of God!" (Mk 10:23). This echoes ancient prophetic challenge to the rich who exploited the poor. (Isa 5:8) Ultimately the restoration of God's rule would not happen without major changes in the administration in Jerusalem. Jesus' confrontations in Jerusalem heighten the tensions between the people and those in power. The death of Jesus symbolizes the requirements of discipleship (Mk 8:34–35). The Gospel ending with empty tomb suggests his followers will continue the struggle: "He is going before you to Galilee" (16:7).

The question of whether parables come from Jesus or later tradition has been debated for decades. Crossan quotes one of the notable parable experts, Bernard Brandon Scott, who asserts, "The burden of proof [falls] on the one who would claim that the originating structure of a parable is not from Jesus." His reasoning is parables are absent in the Old Testament, Hellenistic literature and Rabbinic literature prior to 70 CE. These observations do not prove the parables come from Jesus, but instead challenge the assumption that parables come from the evangelists rather than Jesus (Crossan, J., "The Parables of Jesus," *Interpretation*, July 2002, 56:3, 249).

JESUS AS PROTESTER: CONFRONTATION IN JERUSALEM

Whatever conflicts Jesus had with the religious elite: scribes who came up from Jerusalem (Mk 7) and with some Pharisees (Mk 2 and 3), his entrance to Jerusalem led to his arrest and execution. He entered Jerusalem and challenged how the Temple was being run, thereby protesting Roman control and religious cooperation with Rome.

Jewish tensions with Rome over Jerusalem and the Temple were strong: Josephus notes it was Herod who installed a golden eagle on the Temple, and this helped to cause sedition (c. 4 BCE).

> There also now happened to him [King Herod], among his other calamities, a certain popular sedition . . . (Josephus, *Jewish Wars*, 1.33.2)

> The king [Herod] had erected over the great gate of the temple a large golden eagle, of great value, and had dedicated it to the temple. Now the law forbids those that propose to live according to it, to erect images or representations of any living creature. So these wise men persuaded [their scholars] to pull down the golden eagle . . . (Josephus, *Antiquities*, 17.6.2)

Closer to the time of Jesus, Pilate had erected images of Caesar in Jerusalem (c. 26 CE); this triggered strong protests, and Pilate then removed the images.

> Now Pilate, who was sent as procurator into Judea by Tiberius, sent by night those images of Caesar that are called ensigns into Jerusalem. This excited a very great tumult among the Jews when it was day; for those that were near them were astonished at the sight of them, as indications that their laws were trodden under foot; for those laws do not permit any sort of image to be brought into the city. (Josephus, *Jewish Wars*, 2.9.3; also *Antiquities*, 18.6.2)

In the Temple Mark (also in Mt and Lk) has Jesus quoting Jeremiah: And he taught, and said to them, "Is it not written, 'My house shall be called a house of prayer for all the nations?' But you have made it a den of robbers" (Mk 11:17). Jeremiah has: "Has this house, which bears my Name, become a den of robbers to you? But I have been watching! declares the LORD" (Jeremiah 7:11).

Jeremiah had warned the people in Judah in the context of their behavior relative to the Temple:

Thus says the Lord of hosts, the God of Israel, amend your ways and your doings, and I will let you dwell in this place. Do not trust in these deceptive words: "This is the temple of the Lord, the temple of the Lord, the temple of the Lord."

For if you truly amend your ways and your doings, if you truly execute justice one with another, if you do not oppress the alien, the fatherless or the widow, or shed innocent blood in this place, and if you do not go after other gods to your own hurt, then I will let you dwell in this place, in the land that I gave of old to your fathers forever. (Jeremiah 7:3–7)

Jeremiah says the people need to "execute justice" and not oppress the alien if they want to maintain their Temple.

Since Mark's Jesus quotes Jeremiah, we can assume his message is similar. The Temple is no hiding place for those who practice injustice, oppression, or violence; without the right behavior the Temple would be destroyed (Jer 7:14–15; Ps 78:60). The priests running the Temple would have heard this challenge. The Romans could not have cared less about the moral behavior of the priests. Instead, the Romans would be interested in civil order, and when things ran smoothly, there was money coming to Herod, a client of the Romans.

In Mark 11:11 ff., Jesus curses the fig tree for not having fruit out of season, and it dies. The fig tree is a symbol of the Temple which has not borne fruit. The barrenness of the fig tree expresses the barrenness of the Temple. At the death of Jesus in chapter 15 the Temple veil is torn in two to indicate the passing of the Temple. The destruction of the fig tree is a prophetic gesture bespeaking the destruction of the Temple. Prophets expressed God's message to a community by word and here by deed.

Notice the reaction of the vineyard's tenants and attempted arrest of Jesus (Mk 12:12–13). Who is the owner of the vineyard? God or Herod and the religious elite?

Jesus is depicted as saying that several prophets have been sent to Israel (Isaiah 5 depicts the vineyard as the house of Judah). The rejection of the envoys and of the son of the vineyard owner will lead the owner to deliver the vineyard into the hands of others (12:9). "What will the owner of the vineyard do? He will come and destroy the tenants, and give the vineyard to others."

Imagine this parable to have been written (1a and 1b) after the time of Jesus thus reflecting the mission of Mark's Gospel or (2) composed at the time of and perhaps by Jesus, thus reflecting the mission of Jesus.

Two competing interpretations of this parable depend on the meaning of the owner. Is the owner God or the Temple state?

INTERPRETATIONS 1A AND 1B

The "others" could mean Gentiles. The parable would thus be interpreting the Roman dominance of the land. After another failed Jewish revolt against Romans by Bar Kochba, the name of Judea was changed by Romans to Syria Palestina ("In an effort to wipe out all memory of the bond between the Jews and the land, Hadrian changed the name of the province from Iudaea to Syria-Palestina, a name that became common in non-Jewish literature," Ben-Sasson, H. H., *A History of the Jewish People*, 334). "It seems clear that by choosing a seemingly neutral name—one juxtaposing that of a neighboring province with the revived name of an ancient geographical entity (Palestine), already known from the writings of Herodotus—Hadrian was intending to suppress any connection between the Jewish people and that land" (Lewin, Ariel, *The Archaeology of Ancient Judea and Palestine*, 33). "Aelia Capitolina" was a Roman settlement built upon the ruins of Jerusalem.

(1a) Is the owner God? Is this parable saying God will punish the Jewish leaders ("the chief priests and the scribes and the elders came to him," 11:27; "and they tried to arrest him, but feared the multitude, for they perceived that he had told the parable against them," 12:12) in Jerusalem by sending destruction on Jerusalem?

In O.T. destruction by foreign armies was sometimes interpreted as God's doing:

> I [the Lord] I will make Jerusalem a heap of ruins, a lair of jackals; and I will make the cities of Judah a desolation, without inhabitant. (Jeremiah 9:11)

This destruction was probably at the hands of the Babylonians.

> And now I will tell you what I will do to my vineyard.
> I will remove its hedge, and it shall be devoured;
> I will break down its wall, and it shall be trampled down.
> I will make it a waste; it shall not be pruned or hoed,
> and briers and thorns shall grow up;
> I will also command the clouds that they rain no rain upon it.
> For the vineyard of the Lord of hosts is the house of Israel.
> (Isaiah 5)

This imagery is referring to fall of Northern Kingdom of Israel to the Assyrians.

This position imagines the challenge to come *after* the time of Jesus when Mark's Gospel may be interpreting the destruction of Jerusalem at the hands of the Romans as God's displeasure with Jewish leadership.

Is there anything troublesome about this? Is Jesus' God capable of indiscriminate killing by the destruction of Jerusalem with at least some innocent people in its population?

(1b) A related interpretation: "they tried to arrest him." If "they" is taken to refer to Jews, instead of Jewish leaders, who killed the son of God, and God therefore rejects them. This anti-Jewish interpretation shows a danger of interpreting Jesus in terms of prophecy (Psalm 118, "the stone which the builders rejected has become the cornerstone." See Miller, *Helping Jesus Interpret Prophecy*, 369 ff).

(2) Another interpretation takes the parable as *coming from Jesus, not later* (recall Bernard B. Scott asserting "the burden of proof falls on the one who would claim that the originating structure of the parable is not from Jesus," Crossan, "The Parables of Jesus," *Interpretation*, 249).

The parable is about the tension between the ruled and the rulers. Jesus' opponents are the people running the Temple: In Mk 11 Jesus quotes Jeremiah (ch. 7): "Is it not written, 'My house shall be called a house of prayer for all the nations'? But you have made it a den of robbers." And the chief priests and the scribes heard it and sought a way to destroy him." Jesus' opponents are primarily priests, scribes, and Pharisees (Horsley, *Jesus and the Politics of Roman Palestine*, 48–49, 121). In other words, the parable may envision a restoration of the people to own their land rather than simply a catastrophe. This position holds that Jesus was making this challenge.

Clearly *the parable is against the Judean leaders* (Mk 11:27; 12:12). "They tried to arrest him, . . . for they perceived that he had told the parable against them." If the parable depicts the owner of the vineyard as representing the religious authorities or even Herod with his son as Herod Antipas, then the political/religious authorities would be seen as ruthless enough to destroy the tenants. The tenants are presented as trying to overthrow the rule of the Temple state to get their land back.

The interpretation that God is the owner (#1) presents God as vindictive and murderous (Mk 12:9). The other interpretation of the owner as the religious/political elite (#2) avoids that notion of God and fits with Jesus' challenge to those who have made the Temple a "den of robbers."

LACK OF ACKNOWLEDGMENT

Notice early in Mark's Gospel the lack of recognition given to Jesus by some Pharisees, a group of pious Jews aligned more with law than Temple. Pharisees often receive negative treatment in the New Testament though they were invested in specifying in detail how to love God and how to consecrate ordinary daily activities rather than putting emphasis on Temple sacrifices.

They thus became associated with rules of religious behavior. Chapter 2 of Mark's Gospel and the beginning of chapter 3 contain five hostility stories in which people, largely scribes and Pharisees, are opposed to Jesus and are trying to catch him in some inconsistency or infraction of a religious rule. In each case Jesus is depicted as outsmarting his opponents, and this series of conflicts culminates in 3:6 with the plot to destroy him. Either he is right or the people behind the laws he is breaking are right. Those Pharisees decide he has to be eliminated.

The Pharisees again challenge Jesus in chapter 7 in terms of the behavior of his disciples who eat with hands unwashed, and in chapter 8 they seek to test Jesus by asking for a sign from heaven. (More on Pharisees below, pp. 44–45.)

THE FAMILY

The family of Jesus in Mark's Gospel is presented as wanting to remove him from the public sphere: "And when his family heard it, they went out to seize him, for people were saying, 'He is beside himself'" (Mk 3:21), Later in chapter 3, Mark highlights Jesus' distance from his blood family with the words contrasting those who sit around Jesus inside a house and his blood relatives outside the house: "'Who are my mother and my brothers?'" (Mk 3:31). This same tension applies to his extended family and the people from his local region in Galilee: "'Only in his hometown, among his relatives and in his own house is a prophet without honor'" (Mk 6:4).

THE DISCIPLES

The lack of recognition by Pharisees and by his family begin an important theme, namely misunderstanding. As early as chapter 6, when Jesus walks on the water, Mark has the disciples amazed, "for they had not understood about the loaves; their hearts were hardened" (Mk 6:52). In chapter 8, Mark takes the misunderstanding by the disciples to a high level, even to being ludicrous. They misunderstand Jesus' metaphor of leaven meaning influence and think he is talking about bread. "Why do you discuss the fact that you have no bread? Do you not yet perceive or understand? Are your hearts hardened? Having eyes do you not see, and having ears do you not hear? And do you not remember?" (8:17–18). After all of the misunderstanding by those outside the circle of disciples in the challenges by the religious elites, Jesus asks them who people say he is and then asks Peter his opinion. Peter calls him "Christ," which sounds fine to contemporary ears but carried a largely political meaning in the time of Jesus.

The Bible associates King David, who ruled over a Hebrew kingdom with its capital in Jerusalem about a thousand years before Jesus, with a prophecy uttered by Nathan that establishes a Davidic dynasty "forever." "He is the one who will build a house for my Name, and I will establish the throne of his kingdom forever" (2 Sm 7:13; also Ps 89:4). Since the Hebrew people did not manage to have only descendants of David as rulers (Jer 22:30), the expectation remained, with varying degrees of intensity in different periods of history, for that ruler to be sent by God; this is the hoped-for Messiah or in Greek, *Christos*. Christ meant someone who would be anointed by God to rule Israel.

When Jesus in Mark 8 asks Peter who he thinks Jesus is, Peter says "the Christ." Immediately afterwards Jesus gives a passion prediction announcing he will die shortly. Peter rebukes Jesus (Mk 8:32), and Jesus in turn rebukes Peter, saying he is not on the side of God. Why are they fighting?

The answer is contained in the meaning of "Christ" in the first century. It was the term for the God appointed king, and Jesus was not in any ordinary sense a king. Mark himself gives the reason in the next chapter when Jesus gives a passion prediction leading to misunderstanding. After saying he will be killed, the disciples do not understand (Mark 9:31–2). The misunderstanding motif continues with them discussing who was the greatest. The association with the new king would naturally extend to his close followers, so their expectation would involve acquisition of political power.

The same theme of misunderstanding continues in chapter 10 when Jesus predicts his death a third time: the disciples again request, "'we want you to do for us whatever we ask.' 'What do you want me to do for you?'" he asked. They replied, "'Let one of us sit at your right and the other at your left in your glory.' 'You don't know what you are asking . . . '" (Mark 10:35–38). The disciples are presented as interested in power, which supports the difficulty Peter is having in understanding how Jesus can be the new king and yet speak of impending death. This is hardly a way to kick off a political campaign.

Why would one portray the disciples having so much misunderstanding in the dialogs with Jesus? One literary answer is to give the character Jesus an opportunity to explain himself and his take on what it means to follow

Table 2.1. Passion Prediction

Passion Prediction	Mark 8:31	Mark 9:31	Mark 10:33–34
Misunderstanding	8:32+	9:32–34	10:35–38
Teaching on Discipleship	8:34+	9:35	10:42–44

him. The disciples' misunderstanding is juxtaposed against the teaching on discipleship in chapters 8–10.

Why does this pattern occur? What is Mark trying to accomplish by repeating the pattern of passion prediction followed by misunderstanding, then followed by teaching on discipleship? The answer to this is a key to understanding the unity of Mark's Gospel.

What is the teaching on discipleship in these chapters? Chapter 8:34–35 can hardly be more pointed: "'If anyone would come after me, he must deny himself and take up his cross and follow me. For whoever wants to save his life will lose it, but whoever loses his life for me and for the gospel will save it.'" Discipleship involves self-denial and willingness to lose one's life, either physically, as there was the danger of persecution from both Jews and Romans (Mark 4:16–17; 13:9), or metaphorically. After the disciples are told to lose their life in chapter 8, they pop up with the question about who is the greatest (9:34)!

Discipleship in chapter 9 is about service, not political power or status: "If anyone wants to be first, he must be the very last and the servant of all" (Mark 9:35). In spite of this teaching in chapter 10, the disciples ask Jesus to let them sit at the right and left hand of Jesus in glory. Jesus counters with "'You do not know what you are asking'" and then tells them about discipleship: "Jesus called them together and said, 'You know that those who are regarded as rulers of the Gentiles lord it over them, and their high officials exercise authority over them. Not so with you. Instead, whoever wants to become great among you must be your servant and whoever wants to be first must be slave of all'" (Mk 10:43–44). Teaching on discipleship is given after each passion prediction and misunderstanding ch. 8, 9, 10. The teaching is self-denial and service, and these ideas are related. The cross is a symbol of self-denial and service in as much as Jesus did not put his welfare or self-concern first but rather his mission to challenge the understanding of God and religious practice. An outspoken prophet would face danger in going to Jerusalem, but Jesus is presented as forging ahead. He put his self-interest behind his mission and was arrested and put to death. Self-denial was necessary to enable him to continue to serve.

Why does Mark repeat this pattern of passion prediction, misunderstanding, and teaching on discipleship three times in these three chapters? Evidently this repetition suggests the teaching is important; a fuller appreciation of the pattern comes from examining who recognizes and acknowledges Jesus as Son of God in Mark's Gospel.

ACKNOWLEDGEMENT

In chapter one, the "unclean spirit" inhabiting a man cries out: "I know who you are—the Holy One of God!" (Mark 1:24). A similar knowledge is noted in 3:11. The man possessed by unclean spirits called Legion in chapter 5 similarly identifies Jesus: "What do you want with me, Jesus, Son of the Most High God?" (Mark 5:7).

God is also shown to acknowledge Jesus as His son in chapter 1 at the baptism of Jesus: "And a voice came from heaven: 'You are my Son, whom I love; with you I am well pleased'" (Mark 1:11). The same type of declaration comes at the transfiguration: "A voice came from the cloud: 'This is my Son, whom I love. Listen to him!'" (Mark 9:7).

God and the demons recognize and acknowledge Jesus as son of God, but nearly all of the humans in Mark's Gospel do not. The Pharisees, the family, the townsfolk, later those who have Jesus arrested and killed (11:18; 12:12; 14:60+) all manage to misunderstand that Jesus is God's son. Only one human being in the entire Gospel is given the role of recognizing Jesus as God's son; this is the centurion at the foot of the cross. Here Jesus breathes his last breath, and when the centurion sees this says, "'Surely this man was the Son of God!'" (Mark 15:39).

There is no psychological preparation for this character to finally say what no other human has said throughout this Gospel; he comes out of nowhere. He is given the climactic line despite or because of his lack of religious education; he is after all a Gentile without training in the Hebrew tradition. His important role would appeal to Gentile readers. All he sees is Jesus die and the dead body on the cross. What is Mark saying by this?

The pattern of lack of recognition or acknowledgement of Jesus as Son of God is Mark's way of suggesting how easy it is to misunderstand Jesus. To give the moment of recognition to the centurion who saw no great works of healing or exorcism, who saw no walking on water or multiplication of loaves, is Mark's way of saying the key to understanding Jesus is the cross. Spectacular deeds are fine, but they may not cut through human self-seeking.

The cross has a long history of interpretation, but in Mark's Gospel it is linked to discipleship. In the first response to Peter's misunderstanding in chapter 8, Jesus gives the teaching on discipleship to deny self and to take up one's cross and follow (Mk 8:34). The cross, as a Roman method of killing people, was a real threat to some of Mark's first readers. The cross is also a symbol of self-denial and supports his other teaching on discipleship, namely service. Self-denial is not usually attractive as it goes against ordinary human aspiration. These are the last things people want to hear, self-denial and death. Losing life, aside from its literal meaning, is also a metaphor for self-denial:

"whoever loses his life for me" (Mk 8:35). The added teaching on service from chapters 9 and 10 fills out the meaning. Self-denial is in service of the good of others. While "service" is a bit more palatable, the idea of self-denial can hardly fail to evoke a defense in people. Mark's threefold repetition of the teaching on discipleship is his warning to the reader: don't miss it. It is easy to miss the teaching of Jesus on being one of his followers because what he asks goes against what people usually want.

The lack of acknowledgement on the part of the humans in the Markan Gospel includes a caution to the reader against the deaf spot of not hearing a teaching that asks what people do not want to give. Mark artistically nested the stories of passion prediction, misunderstanding, and teaching on discipleship between two stories of blindness: 8:22+ and 10:46. Who is blind?

One would do well to consider another implication of recognition and the lack of recognition of Jesus as Son of God on the part of the characters in this Gospel. None of the people who saw any great works of power such as healing, exorcism, walking on water, multiplication of loaves or even transfiguration are shown to acknowledge Jesus' identity as Son of God. The disciples saw Jesus transfigured, but they are left without understanding (Mk 9:32). Even the empty tomb leaves the witnesses filled with fear (16:8). The disciples' attraction to power, however natural, does not lead to the kind of acknowledgement given by the centurion who sees Jesus on the cross. The only place in Mark's Gospel where Jesus appears to accept the title of "Christ" is when he is completely powerless, when any fantasy about his political career would dissolve, namely when he is under arrest and being interrogated by the high priest (14:61–62). Jesus' acceptance of "Christ" in Mark 14 is far removed from someone who is to take over the government. The Gospel thus keeps wonderworking as part of Jesus' profile, but it gives greater emphasis to his teaching on self-denial and service.

HIDDENNESS AND SECRECY

A frequent topic in Markan studies is hiddenness. We have seen thus far that Jesus was not recognized by most people in the Gospel which in and of itself establishes him as hidden. There is an additional element to hiddenness, namely he asks demons and some of the people he has healed not to tell anyone. Jesus in Mark enjoins silence upon the demons. In Mark 1:25, he commands the unclean spirit to "be silent." "He also drove out many demons, but he would not let the demons speak because they knew who he was" (Mk 1:34). He orders the unclean spirits in chapter 3 not to make Jesus known (v. 12).

As for those healed, "He gave strict orders not to let anyone know about this" in 5:43. In a couple of instances he asks for silence and is immediately disobeyed. "'See that you don't tell this to anyone . . . ' Instead, he went out and began to talk freely, spreading the news. As a result, Jesus could no longer enter a town openly but stayed outside in lonely places" in 1:43–5. The same scenario occurs in chapter 7: "Jesus commanded them not to tell anyone. But the more he did so, the more they kept talking about it" (7:36). In the last couple of examples, the command to secrecy has no effect, as people broadcast the wonder of Jesus' deeds; this ties into the lack of understanding on the part of the characters. These passages raise the question of why? What about Jesus' ministry was better kept secret?

Two related answers fit the question and explain secrecy in terms of a desire to avoid confusion. First of all, the confusion about his political aspirations may have led him to want a low profile. Roman domination including persecution would likely be a major factor in encouraging secrecy among Jesus' followers and Mark's audience. Roman rule was strong, and Jewish resistance would be fruitless. Mark would not want his people spreading any destabilizing notions that Jesus and his followers would want to replace Roman rule. It is also absurd to believe public acts of healing and exorcism could remain secret. To attempt to attribute this element of secrecy to the psychology of the historical Jesus (Marcus, Joel, 525+) is to assume more knowledge than contemporary interpreters have.

A second reason for secrecy may derive from the interest of Mark to highlight the importance of the cross over any healing activity. There were other healers or wonderworkers in the ancient world, and perhaps Mark does not want Jesus to be reduced to another wonderworker. This idea that Mark was distinguishing Jesus from Hellenistic wonderworkers arose in the 1970s and has generated a controversy that is not over. (For bibliography see Dwyer, Timothy, p. 27, fn 5.)

Healing in the ancient world outside of the parameters of contemporary understandings of medicine occurs in a variety of cultures related to Biblical history. Tacitus describes the Roman Emperor Vespasian (9–79 CE) healing with spittle:

> In the months during which Vespasian was waiting at Alexandria for the periodical return of the summer gales and settled weather at sea, many wonders occurred which seemed to point him out as the object of the favour of heaven and of the partiality of the Gods. One of the common people of Alexandria, well known for his blindness, threw himself at the Emperor's knees, and implored him with groans to heal his infirmity. This he did by the advice of the God Serapis, whom this nation, devoted as it is to many superstitions, worships more than any other divinity. He begged Vespasian that he would deign to moisten his

cheeks and eye-balls with his spittle. Another with a diseased hand, at the coun-
sel of the same God, prayed that the limb might feel the print of a Caesar's foot.
At first Vespasian ridiculed and repulsed them. They persisted; and he, though
on the one hand he feared the scandal of a fruitless attempt, yet, on the other,
was induced by the entreaties of the men and by the language of his flatterers
to hope for success. At last he ordered that the opinion of physicians should
be taken, as to whether such blindness and infirmity were within the reach of
human skill. They discussed the matter from different points of view. 'In the one
case,' they said, 'the faculty of sight was not wholly destroyed, and might return,
if the obstacles were removed; in the other case, the limb, which had fallen into
a diseased condition, might be restored, if a healing influence were applied;
such, perhaps, might be the pleasure of the Gods, and the Emperor might be
chosen to be the minister of the Divine will; at any rate, all the glory of a suc-
cessful remedy would be Caesar's, while the ridicule of failure would fall on the
sufferers.' And so Vespasian, supposing that all things were possible to his good
fortune, and that nothing was any longer past belief, with a joyful countenance,
amid the intense expectation of the multitude of bystanders, accomplished what
was required. The hand was instantly restored to its use, and the light of day
again shone upon the blind. Persons actually present attest both facts, even now
when nothing is to be gained by falsehood. (*The Histories*, 4:81)

It is uncertain if this text is straightforward or filled with sarcasm, but for our
purpose, it suggests Jesus was not alone in this method.
    Jewish testimony to exorcism:

[Solomon] also composed the kind of incantations by which (spiritual) disorders
are alleviated. And he left his posterity the way to use exorcisms to drive away
demons so that they never return. This type of cure is exceptionally powerful
among our own people down to this day (c. 90 CE).

As you may know, I have observed a man by the name of Eleazar free a
demon-possessed victim in the presence of Vespasian [the emperor], his sons
and tribunes, and a host of other military personnel. This is how he went about it.

He would hold a ring to the nose of the possessed victim—a ring that had one
of those roots prescribed by Solomon under its seal—and then, as the victim got
a whiff of the root, he would draw the demon out through the victim's nostrils.
The victim would collapse on the spot and (Eleazar) would adjure it never again
to enter him, invoking Solomon by name and reciting incantations Solomon
had composed.

Since Eleazar was always determined to captivate his audience and demonstrate
he possessed this power, he would place a cup or basin full of water not far
from the victim and would order the demon to tip these vessels over on the way

out and thus demonstrate to the onlookers that it had actually taken leave of the victim. (Josephus, *Antiquities*, 8.5)

Pagan testimony to exorcism:

As [Apollonius] was discussing libations, there was a youth nearby who had such a name for luxury and vulgarity that by then there were even street songs about him . . .

Apollonius was speaking about libations and told them not to drink from this cup but to keep it untouched and unused for the gods. But when he told them also to put handles on the cup and (in the libation) to pour it over these—since men are less apt to drink (there)—, the youth drowned out his word with loud and course laughter.

Looking up at him, [Apollonius] said:

"These insults are not from you but from the demon that drives you without your knowing it."

The youth was in fact demon-possessed, for he laughed at things that no one else did. And then he would change to weeping without having any reason to. And he would talk and sing to himself. Now, the people thought that it was the unruliness of youth that led him to do these things. But it was the demon acting. And he seemed to be drunk only because he was then drinking.

Apollonius stared at him; and the phantom started uttering sounds of fear and rage, like those who are burnt and tortured. And the phantom promised to leave the youth alone and never take possession of people again. But speaking with anger like a master to a slave who is unstable, mischievous, shameless, and so forth, (Apollonius) ordered him to depart and to provide proof (that he had done so).

[The demon] said:

"I will knock down that statue," pointing to one of those on the royal porch. When the statue first shook and then fell, there was more commotion and applause at the marvel than anyone could write about. But the youth just rubbed his eyes, as if he was waking up and saw the sun's rays. And he won the attention over everyone who turned to him. For he no longer seemed vulgar, nor did he cast his eyes wildly about. But he returned to his natural self, as if he had been medicated. And he threw away the gowns and dresses of Sybarites and developed a love for a rough shirt and cloak and modeled his behavior on that of Apollonius. (Philostratus [c. 170–c. 247], *Life of Apollonius of Tyana*, 4.20)

John Meier distinguishes magic from miracle in the canonical Gospels. Characteristics of miracles in the Gospels include faith, trust, love; a person is in need and asks for Divine help. Sometimes Jesus takes the initiative. Jesus accompanies the miracle with intelligible words and sometimes with gestures with no lengthy incantations or amulets. The power of God is not coerced. Jesus' action is within the context of the Father's will (Gethsemane) and mission. No one is punished by miracles. (This contrasts with Gnostic presentations of Jesus, where, for example, Jesus kills a boy who is interfering with his play in the *Infancy Gospel of Thomas*, Meier, 548.)

The main point here is Jesus was a healer and exorcist, but there were others. In Mark's Gospel none of those who witnessed healing or exorcism proclaimed him Son of God. Mark is not wanting Jesus to be reduced to the level of another wonderworker. Healing power attracted people, but Jesus' message about discipleship was not about acquiring power (Mk 8–10).

One may connect healing and exorcism with the desperation experienced by peasants under Roman occupation. Horsley surveys numerous African responses to invasions by alien forces which generated illnesses and spirit possessions which in turn spawned exorcisms (Horsley, *Jesus and the Politics of Roman Palestine*, 87–90). "The Tonga along the Zambezi River were invaded by spirits with names such as *maregimenti* and *mapolis* (clearly representations of military regiments and the police) at the height of the invasion of the military state." I had a student who had suffered sexual abuse as a child. The memories of that abuse were so horrendous that they were unconsciously screened out of the center of her consciousness. As an adult she heard voices that encouraged her to commit suicide. (She was diagnosed as having multiple personality disorder today called dissociative identity disorder.) Those voices gave expression to her desperation. I mention the experience of this student to make the point that sometimes social situations generate self-destructive behavior. Jesus as healer was dealing with a society deeply disturbed by foreign occupation and oppression by the religious elite.

For the purpose of understanding Mark's Gospel, it is helpful to remember the context of healing in the time of Jesus. Mark includes these great works, but his emphases on Jesus as recognized on the cross and discipleship as taking up one's cross leads him to somewhat downplay the significance of such healings.

DEATH OF JESUS IN MARK

There are many pointers to the death of Jesus in Mark. No matter how many times I quote: Mark's Gospel has been called a passion narrative with an extended introduction, students never chuckle. The line comes from Martin

Kahler's *The So-called Historical Jesus and the Historic Biblical Christ*, 80, n 11). This simply means much of the Gospel points to Jesus' death. This topic can serve to pull together loose threads.

A useful exercise is to read through the Gospel looking for pointers to Jesus' death: Chapters 2, 3: hostility stories culminating in 3:6 plot to destroy Jesus; ch. 8, 9, 10 passion predictions; 11:18 plot to kill him after confronting money changers in the Temple; 12:12 plot to arrest Jesus after parable of vineyard. The many pointers to the death of Jesus reinforce the thesis of this chapter that Mark presents the cross of Christ as the key to understanding Jesus and the meaning of Christian discipleship.

SON OF GOD AND MESSIAH?

While scholars debate the exact intended audience for Mark's Gospel, it is the case that nearly all early readers and hearers would have lived under Roman rule. Julius Caesar was declared a god, and his adopted son Augustus was thereby "son of God," which was accordingly reflected on Roman coins, in Roman inscriptions, and in Roman literature. Is Mark giving a competing theology to that of the Romans? As Caesar Augustus was "son of God" in virtue of his military conquests that helped to establish *Pax Romana*, Jesus is a son of God who is not about political power and military might. He is a victim, not a conqueror. Without ignoring this Roman context, the ones who call Jesus son of God in Mark are God, the evil spirits, and the centurion, as well as the author of Mark's Gospel (Mk 1:1). Jesus himself is portrayed as accepting the title, though he calls himself "son of man" when interrogated by the high priest: "Again the high priest asked him, "Are you the Christ, the Son of the Blessed?" And Jesus said, "I am . . . " (Mk 14:61–62) Here Jesus accepts a title which has theological and political implications when it is clear that he is powerless and not about to take over the government.

"Messiah" at the time of Jesus was associated with conquest as well. O.T. prophets speak of a messiah who is related to king David who was a military victor (2 Sm 22:44–51). In exile Ezekiel writes of the messiah as a descendent of David who will rule like a shepherd:

> And I will set up over them one shepherd, my servant David, and he shall feed them: he shall feed them and be their shepherd. And I, the LORD, will be their God, and my servant David shall be prince among them; I, the LORD, have spoken. (Ezk 34:23–24)

Jeremiah predicts there will be a messiah who will be a righteous king:

Behold, the days are coming, says the LORD, when I will raise up for David a righteous Branch, and he shall reign as king and deal wisely, and shall execute justice and righteousness in the land. In his days Judah will be saved, and Israel will dwell securely. (Jer 23:5–6)

Aside from these gentler associations with "messiah," messianism shortly before the time of Jesus was revived with Roman rule, as shown by the Psalms of Solomon.

Psalms of Solomon 17 is aimed against Roman rule especially under Pompey:

Behold, O Lord, and raise up unto them their king, the son of David, At the time in the which Thou seest, O God, that he may reign over Israel Thy servant And gird him with strength, that he may shatter unrighteous rulers, And that he may purge Jerusalem from nations that trample (her) down to destruction. Wisely, righteously he shall thrust out sinners from (the) inheritance, He shall destroy the pride of the sinner as a potter's vessel. With a rod of iron he shall break in pieces all their substance, He shall destroy the godless nations with the word of his mouth; At his rebuke nations shall flee before him. (Ps Sol 17)

The Psalms of Solomon (circa 1st century BCE) appear to be written in part against Pompey's Roman rule (See Atkinson) and give a picture of the messiah just prior to the New Testament. Pompey had invaded Jerusalem, had damaged part of the Temple, and had desecrated the Holy of Holies (Josephus, *Antiquities*, 14.4.2–4). Crassus later plundered the treasure in the Holy of Holies (*Antiquities*, 13.7.1). In the Psalms of Solomon, the messiah is militant (see above Ps of Sol 17) and was expected to defeat the Romans.

Similarly, in the Dead Sea Scrolls in several places, the messiah will conquer the foreign (most likely the Roman) ruler. The War Scroll 4Q285 indicates the Davidic messiah would kill the foreigner, the *Kittim* (generally meaning "Romans") in the Dead Sea Scrolls:

Isaiah the prophet: [The thickets of the forest] will be cut down with an axe and Lebanon by a majestic one will f]all. And there shall come forth a shoot from the stump of Jesse the Branch of David and they will enter into judgement with and the Prince of the Congregation, the Bran[ch of David] will kill him by stroke]s and by wounds. And a Priest [of renown (?)] will command the s]lai[n] of the Kitti[m]

(Transcription and translation by Vermes, G., http://www.piney.com/warrule .html; see Atkinson for context and other references. This text has been interpreted in a variety of ways. See Vermes, "The Oxford Forum for Qumran Research: Seminar on the Rule of War from Cave 4 (4Q285)," *Journal of Jewish Studies* 43, 85–90.)

The point remains that in several places in the Dead Sea Scrolls the Messiah was triumphant with using violence: 4Q161, fragments 8–10,16, 20–21 also 1QSb 5:20–29.

The idea of messiah at the time of Jesus as reflected in the Dead Sea Scrolls and the Psalms of Solomon can be understood as a Jewish answer, if not counterpart, to the Roman ruler. God would bring victory to the Davidic messiah over the foreign invaders (Atkinson).

Other books in Jewish tradition have the messiah as a judge and a killer. 2 Baruch and 4 Ezra are difficult to date so their relevance in contextualizing messianic belief at the time of the N.T. is not strong. They simply reinforce the Jewish picture of messiah after most of the texts of the Hebrew Bible were written.

2 Baruch 72 has the messiah as a slayer:

> The time of my messiah is come, he shall both summon all the nations, and some of them he shall spare, and some of them he shall slay.

4 Ezra 12:32–34 also depicts the messiah as a judge and a slayer who will nevertheless deliver his people within his borders:

> [32] this is the messiah whom the Most High has kept until the end of days, who will arise from the posterity of David, and will come and speak to them; he will denounce them for their ungodliness and for their wickedness, and will cast up before them their contemptuous dealings.

> [33] For first he will set them living before his judgment seat, and when he has reproved them, then he will destroy them.

> [34] But he will deliver in mercy the remnant of my people, those who have been saved throughout my borders, and he will make them joyful until the end comes, the day of judgment, of which I spoke to you at the beginning. (4 Ezra 12)

(For additional discussion see Allison, Dale, *Constructing Jesus*, 252.)

Aside from violence, in the Dead Sea Scrolls, there is also language of a messiah who brings the "good news":

> [The hea]vens and the earth will listen to His messiah, and none therein will stray from the commandments of the holy ones. Seekers of the Lord, strengthen yourselves in His service! All you hopeful in (your) heart, will you not find the Lord in this? For the Lord will consider the pious (*hasidim*) and call the righteous by name. Over the poor His spirit will hover and will renew the faithful with His power. And He will glorify the pious on the throne of the eternal Kingdom. He who liberates the captives, restores sight to the blind,

straightens the b[ent] And f[or] ever I will cleav[ve to the h]opeful and in His mercy. . . . And the fr[uit . . .] will not be delayed for anyone. And the Lord will accomplish glorious things which have never been as [He . . .] For He will heal the wounded, and revive the dead and bring good news to the poor. . . . He will lead the uprooted and knowledge . . . and smoke. (Wise, Michael O., translation of 4Q521 http://clas-pages.uncc.edu/james-tabor/archaeology-and-the-dead-sea -scrolls/the-signs-of-the-messiah-4q521/)

This text shows a link in Jewish literature (from approx. 250 BCE to 68 CE) between belief in a messiah and "good news." (For an early reference to this link between messiah and good news in the Dead Sea Scrolls, see Aune, David E., 161–165.)

In addition to the element of violence in Psalm of Solomon 17, the messiah is associated with judgement:

He shall destroy the pride of the sinner as a potter's vessel (24). With a rod of iron he shall break in pieces all their substance (21). He shall destroy the godless nations with the word of his mouth (25). At his rebuke nations shall flee before him, And he shall reprove sinners for the thoughts of their heart (28) (26). And he shall gather together a holy people, whom he shall lead in righteousness. And he shall judge the tribes of the people that has been sanctified by the Lord his God. (http://wesley.nnu.edu/sermons-essays-books/noncanonical-literature/ noncanonical-literature-ot-pseudepigrapha/the-psalms-of-solomon/)

The obvious difficulty with associating Jesus with the term "messiah": He was not victorious over his enemies in a military sense. Jesus in the Gospels is not associated with military victory over Romans. Later Christianity of the Book of Revelation turns away from the non-violent Jesus and embraces the imagery of a militant (see Rev 6 and 19, e.g., "From his mouth issues a sharp sword with which to smite the nations, and he will rule them with a rod of iron; he will tread the wine press of the fury of the wrath of God the Almighty," Rev 19). Mark's Gospel is not entirely comfortable with the term messiah. Remember Jesus' argument with Peter in Chapter 8 after Peter calls him "messiah." Jesus in Mark does not "smite" or "destroy" or "kill." This despite Mark 1:1, where messiah is used as part of Jesus' compound name in some, not all, manuscripts, unlike the rest of Mark where it is a title (see Croy, N. Clayton, 115). Later we will see that Matthew's Gospel is more at home with messiah, though with transformed meaning.

Jesus in Mark is persecuted just as many of his readers. Jesus' response was service, and Mark is advising his followers to focus on service with no implication about toppling Roman rule.

Chapter 3

Matthew's Portrait of Jesus

Fulfillment of Jewish Hope, Teacher of Superior Righteousness, Messiah, Son of God, Founder of the Church, Preacher of the Kingdom of God

Key questions to pose of the text of Matthew's Gospel:

1. What in Matthew's Gospel would lead you to think Matthew was of Jewish background?
2. What is the key line in the Sermon on the Mount?
3. Why do you think Matthew has Jesus' sermon on a mount (Mt 5:1) since Luke has the sermon on a plain (Lk 6:17)?
4. What is Jesus' attitude toward the Mosaic Law as presented by Matthew?
5. Contrast the crucifixion of Jesus in Mark and Matthew.
6. What are the main Old Testament texts in the background of Mt 27:37–54?
7. Compare and contrast the following texts in terms of the disciples: Mk 8:14–21 with Mt 16:5–12 and Mk 6:52 with Mt 14:33.
8. How specifically do the infancy narrative, the Sermon on the Mount, the parables (ch. 13) and community regulations (ch. 18) influence the portrayal of Jesus?

Discussion questions:

1. What might Jesus or his disciples reasonably have expected to be accomplished by going to the Jerusalem Temple?
2. What in Mt 25 resonates with and challenges contemporary Christians?

39

Matthew's Gospel is longer than Mark's and contains an infancy narrative (ch. 1–2), the Sermon on the Mount (ch. 5–7) along with the Lord's Prayer, a long section of parables (ch. 13), and a section on community regulations (ch. 18), all of which influence the portrayal of Jesus. This chapter will include overlap with some of Mark's Gospel, but will not repeat all that Matthew's Gospel has in common with Mark's. The main focus will be on what distinguishes this Gospel from the others.

Jesus' conflict with the Temple state (including both the religious elite, the Herodians and above them the Romans) begins as early as the infancy narrative as Herod wants to kill the newborn king of the Jews, Jesus (2:3–13).

In contrast to the Temple state with its oppressive measures, Jesus brings healings, exorcism, and forgiveness as part of the kingdom of God. The values of this new community include blessings on the poor in sprit, the merciful, the pure of heart and those who hunger for righteousness (Mt 5:3–8); treating others as one would want to be treated (7:12); and freedom from worry (Mt 6).

Chapters 11–18 (similar to Mark's Gospel) show Jesus' attempts to bring God's healing (esp. ch. 8–9), freedom from unclean spirits(Mt 8:28+, 12:22+), forgiveness (6:2+; 9:12+; 18:21+; 18:35) and even feeding (Mt 8; 14; 15) of people in need and who are burdened (11:28–30). He continually meets with opposition from those who live according to another kingdom. Matthew includes several parables in ch. 13 which suggest hidden (like yeast) and unexpected growth of the influence of God.

Beginning with ch. 19 Jesus' conflict with the Temple state comes to a head, and the Roman official condemns him to death (ch. 27). The resurrection shows God's power overcomes the power of the Temple state. Matthew envisions the kingdom of God spreading to all nations (ch. 28). (For more see Warren Carter.)

ECONOMIC CONCERNS

Jesus is preaching the presence and dawning of the kingdom of God. The kingdom of God in the Lord's prayer is not primarily about going to heaven but rather establishing God's kingdom on earth: "Your kingdom come . . . on earth as in heaven" (Mt 6:10). God's rule has some economic implications.

DEBT

Therefore the kingdom of heaven may be compared to a king who wished to settle accounts with his servants. When he began the reckoning, one was brought to him who owed him ten thousand talents; and as he could not pay, his lord ordered him to be sold, with his wife and children and all that he had, and payment to be made. So the servant fell on his knees, imploring him, "Lord, have patience with me, and I will pay you everything." And out of pity for him the lord of that servant released him and forgave him the debt. But that same servant, as he went out, came upon one of his fellow servants who owed him a hundred denarii; and seizing him by the throat he said, "Pay what you owe." So his fellow servant fell down and besought him, "Have patience with me, and I will pay you." He refused and went and put him in prison till he should pay the debt. When his fellow servants saw what had taken place, they were greatly distressed, and they went and reported to their lord all that had taken place. Then his lord summoned him and said to him, "You wicked servant! I forgave you all that debt because you besought me; and should not you have had mercy on your fellow servant, as I had mercy on you?" And in anger his lord delivered him to the jailers, till he should pay all his debt. So also my heavenly Father will do to every one of you, if you do not forgive your brother from your heart. (Mt 18:23–35)

According to this parable debtors could be sold into slavery (along with his family) or put in prison. Many people in Jesus' society were debtors. The Sermon on the Mount reflects the perilous situation facing debtors.

Make friends quickly with your accuser, while you are going with him to court, lest your accuser hand you over to the judge, and the judge to the guard, and you be put in prison; truly, I say to you, you will never get out till you have paid the last penny. (Mt 5:25)

The Lord's prayer shares with this parable and the line in the Sermon on the Mount the message that as one forgives debts so will one be forgiven.

And forgive us our debts, as we also have forgiven our debtors. (Mt 6:12)

The Lord's Prayer in the context of Jesus' society, where many people were poor and in debt, petitions for food, debt relief and justice.

Food: "Give us this day our daily bread" (Mt 6:11) reflects Jesus' concern for feeding in the multiplication of loaves stories (Mk 6 and 8)

Debt relief: "And forgive us our debts" (Mt 6:11)

Justice: "And forgive us our debts, As we also have forgiven our debtors" (Mt 6:11–12)

The prayer asks Jesus' followers to forgive and to be treated by God the way they have treated others.

In that society, forgiving debtors is largely about monetary debt to rich owners. Richard Horsley focuses on the meaning of the Lord's Prayer in the context of the poor in Israel:

[Jesus'] proclamation of the presence of the Kingdom of God is directed to the poor, hungry, and indebted. To people who may have assumed they were cursed by God because of their poverty and sickness he declared, "Blessed are the poor, for yours is the kingdom of God, Blessed are those who hunger, for they shall be filled." In its more original form, following the Lukan length but the Matthean wording: "Father: May thy kingdom come, give us today, day by day our subsistence bread. Forgive us our debts as we herewith forgive our debtors. And lead us not to the test." What is the kingdom of God about: subsistence food and freedom from debilitating indebtedness to the creditors, who were probably Antipas' officers, the wealthy and powerful based in Sepphoris and Tiberias. One of the most fundamental features of the Mosaic covenant tradition was the provision that every seventh year debts would be canceled. The kingdom for which Jesus is teaching the people to pray will involve the cancellation of debts, just as was supposed to be done following the Mosaic covenant. Note in the prayer the people, in anticipation that God is about to act on their behalf to cancel their debts, promise that they "herewith forgive" their debtors. Keep that in mind when we come to "love your enemies." (https://archive.archaeology.org /online/features/romanworld/)

With this economic perspective in mind, the section of Mt 25 on care for the needy fits with the thrust of Matthew's version of the Lord's Prayer:

"I was hungry and you gave me food, I was thirsty and you gave me drink, I was a stranger and you welcomed me, I was naked and you clothed me, I was sick and you visited me, I was in prison and you came to me." Then the righteous will answer him, "Lord, when did we see thee hungry and feed thee, or thirsty and give thee drink? And when did we see thee a stranger and welcome thee, or naked and clothe thee? And when did we see thee sick or in prison and visit thee?" And the King will answer them, "Truly, I say to you, as you did it to one of the least of these my brethren, you did it to me." Then he will say to those at his left hand, "Depart from me, you cursed, into the eternal fire prepared for the devil and his angels; for I was hungry and you gave me no food, I was thirsty and you gave me no drink, I was a stranger and you did not welcome me, naked and you did not clothe me, sick and in prison and you did not visit me." Then they also will answer, "Lord, when did we see thee hungry or thirsty or a stranger or naked or sick or in prison, and did not minister to thee?" Then he will answer them, "Truly, I say to you, as you did it not to one of the least of these, you did it not to me." And they will go away into eternal punishment, but the righteous into eternal life.

PHARISEES TAKING OVER LEADERSHIP

The destruction of the Temple in Jerusalem in 70 CE (hinted at in a parable in 22:7) caused the loss of Temple worship, where animal sacrifice was offered. Without the Temple, Jewish religion needed to be recast. The author of Matthew's Gospel helps with this adjustment by presenting Jesus as de-emphasizing ritual sacrifice: his presentation of Jesus follows Hosea: "But go and learn what this means: 'I desire mercy, not sacrifice.' For I have not come to call the righteous, but sinners" (Mt 9:13). Matthew 12:7 says, "If you had known what these words mean, 'I desire mercy, not sacrifice, you would not have condemned the innocent.'" Only in Matthew are the words "not sacrifice" added and show at least Matthew's situation after the destruction of the Temple. With the destruction of the Temple, the priests were largely put out of business; to this day Judaism has not recovered priesthood. This de-emphasis is not totally a result of the destruction of the Temple; it may also reflect attitudes in Matthew's community which may in turn resonate with Jesus' teaching. Jesus in Matthew's Gospel is not completely opposed to Temple ritual. In chapter 5:23–24, Jesus refers to someone offering in the Temple: "If you are offering your gift at the altar, and there remember that your brother has something against you, leave your gift there before the altar and go; first be reconciled to your brother, and then come and offer your gift." This presupposes participation in Temple ritual by some of Matthew's audience. These lines also show Jesus' emphasis is on reconciliation with a brother without which the ritual action is to be avoided. (Davies and Allison, 518)

Jesus as a prophet for justice, as in Mark, continues to challenge the religious elite in the style of Hebrew Prophets. In Mt 23 there is a series of "woes" reminiscent of the prophetic "woes" of Jeremiah:

> Woe to him who builds his house by unrighteousness, and his upper rooms by injustice; who makes his neighbor serve him for nothing, and does not give him his wages; . . . you have eyes and heart only for your dishonest gain, for shedding innocent blood, and for practicing oppression and violence. (Jeremiah 22: 13–17)

> Woe to you scribes and Pharisees, hypocrites! For you tithe mint, dill, and cumin, and have neglected the weightier matters of the law: justice and mercy and faith (Mt 23:23).

> Woe to you, scribes and Pharisees, hypocrites! for you build the tombs of the prophets and adorn the monuments of the righteous, saying, "If we had lived in the days of our fathers, we would not have taken part with them in shedding the blood of the prophets. Thus you witness against yourselves, that you are sons of those who murdered the prophets." (Mt 23:29–31)

Denouncing injustice and calling for justice resonate through Hebrew prophetic traditions, as well as Jesus' conflict with scribes and Pharisees.

After Jesus the antagonism grew as "church" and "synagogue" became competing institutions. Matthew uses "their synagogues" more than the other Synoptics, suggesting that tension between early Christianity and synagogues was not unique to Matthew but nevertheless more of an issue.

> Matthew 6:2: Thus, when you give alms, sound no trumpet before you, as the hypocrites do in the synagogues and in the streets, that they may be praised by men. Truly, I say to you, they have received their reward.

> Matthew 6:5: And when you pray, you must not be like the hypocrites; for they love to stand and pray in the synagogues and at the street corners, that they may be seen by men. Truly, I say to you, they have received their reward.

> Matthew 9:35: And Jesus went about all the cities and villages, teaching in their synagogues and preaching the gospel of the kingdom, and healing every disease and every infirmity.

> Matthew 10:17: Beware of men; for they will deliver you up to councils, and flog you in their synagogues.

While Matthew's emphases on struggle with Pharisees may have come from Jesus' ongoing prophetic confrontation, evident in the whole ch. 23, the developing tension with "their synagogues" reflects more of a distinction and later distance between church and synagogue. Matthew has references to being flogged in synagogues: Mt 10:17; 23:34, nevertheless Jesus preached in synagogues (Mt 4:23; 9:35; Mk 1:21; 3:1, etc.) as did Paul (Acts 13:5, 43, etc.). Institutional borderlines took time to emerge.

The Pharisees took over the leadership of Judaism and eventually led to the re-expression of Jewish life through rabbinic writings known as Mishna and Talmud. The Pharisees, largely a group of pious laymen, helped to make Jewish life comprehensible without the Temple by focusing on the consecration of everyday activities. For Pharisees, the family table was the table of the Lord. Their attempt to specify how to love God in everyday life led some, especially Christians, to associate them with legalism, but they were actually attempting to democratize religion by taking religious practice out of the control of the priests and those who made their living through the Temple.

It would be a mistake to generalize and regard all Pharisees as bad or legalistic or worthy of confrontation. In the highly charged atmosphere of the New Testament, one would not expect to read much that is positive about Pharisees. There are, however, a few texts that work against sweeping generalizations. A Pharisee named Nicodemus in John 3 showed himself to be open minded and willing to dialog with Jesus. A prominent Pharisee, Gamaliel, in Acts

15:33–39, advised an angry crowd who wanted to kill Peter and other apostles to back off, thus saving their lives. In Luke's Gospel a Pharisee attempted to save Jesus' life: "some Pharisees came, and said to him, "Get away from here, for Herod wants to kill you" (Lk 13:31). (For more see Neusner, 391, and Pawlikowski, 85+.) A related group, the scribes, are presented in largely negative terms in the New Testament, but one is receptive to Jesus: "Teacher, I will follow you wherever you go" (Mt 8:19).

FULFILLMENT OF JEWISH HOPE

While Pharisees were claiming that their lifestyle and teachings were the fulfillment of Jewish hope, Matthew's Gospel was claiming that Jesus was the fulfillment of Jewish hope. This meant that Matthew's Gospel and the Pharisees were competing for the same audience for recruits. Matthew's emphasis on the distance between his community and those of the Pharisees shows up in Mt 6:2; 6:5; 9:35 and 10:17. This negative language fed the anti-Semitism of later centuries. Matthew's Gospel is competing for market share, not trying to eliminate a people or a religion. If the Pharisees are inviting people to synagogues to learn the future of Jewish life, Matthew's Gospel is saying Jesus is the way of the future.

Matthew connects Jesus repeatedly to Jewish prophecy. Unlike Mark's Gospel, the first two chapters are peppered with references to fulfillment of prophecy. I count the use of fulfillment in relation to law and prophets 14 times in Matthew's Gospel (see especially chapters 1 and 2); fulfillment of scripture occurs only once in Mark (Mk 14:49) and four times in Luke.

Matthew's use of prophecy is sometimes forced. Micah reads "But you, Bethlehem-Ephrathah *least* among the clans of Judah" (Micah 5:1). Matthew changes the text to read: "And you, Bethlehem, land of Judah, *are by no means least* among the rulers of Judah" (Mt 2:6). Most likely Mt changes the description of Bethlehem from an unimportant town to one that is "by no means least," the birthplace of Jesus the messiah.

"And he went and dwelt in a city called Nazareth, that what was spoken by the prophets might be fulfilled, 'He shall be called a Nazarene.'" The problem is there is no such prophecy; Nazareth is not mentioned in the Old Testament. (For numerous instances of such forced prophecy see Robert Miller, *Helping Jesus Interpret Prophecy*.)

Despite Matthew's use of prophecy, these examples of forced prophecies suggest that using prophecy is not a solid contemporary basis for understanding Jesus.

Supporting the notion of fulfillment is a minor theme of likeness to Moses. This Moses motif appears in the infancy narrative where Jesus as a baby is under threat of death from the king but escapes. Moses as an infant similarly is under threat of death from Pharaoh but escapes (Ex 1–2). Moses, patriarchal symbol of the Torah or Jewish Law contained in the first five books of the Hebrew Bible, gave the Law while on the mountain. Jesus in the Sermon on the Mount (Mt 5–7) gives a new interpretation of the Law.

Jesus in the Sermon on the Mount announces he is not abolishing but fulfilling the law (Mt 5:17+) and proceeds to quote some laws associated with Moses but then stretches them in a more demanding direction. "You have heard that it was said to the people long ago, 'Do not murder, and anyone who murders will be subject to judgment,' but I tell you that anyone who is angry with his brother will be subject to judgment" (Mt 5:21–22). In Greek the language "but I tell you" is *ego de lego*, and these words occur six times in Matthew chapter 5 (vv. 22, 28, 32, 34, 39, 44). The significance of this language is about Jesus' moral authority. He is taking the highest authority of his culture and putting his own words above it. In this way he is not only like Moses who gave the law on the mountain, but he is depicted as greater than Moses with his willingness to put his own words above the Law of Moses and to give a more demanding interpretation of moral life.

This respect for Jewish law shows up also in Matthew's removal of "thus he declared all foods clean" from Mk 7:19 when discussing the traditions of the elders in Mt 15. He is addressing Jewish Christians and side steps this challenge to kosher dietary rules.

TEACHER OF SUPERIOR RIGHTEOUSNESS

Jesus in the Sermon on the Mount is the teacher of superior righteousness. Not only does he push beyond existing moral guidelines, but he also issues a warning, challenging people to go beyond the righteousness of the scribes and Pharisees. "'For I tell you that unless your righteousness surpasses that of the Pharisees and the teachers of the law, you will certainly not enter the kingdom of heaven'" (Mt 5:20). The highest expression of this righteousness in the Sermon is love based on God's indiscriminate love of all people, both the just and the unjust (Mt 5:43–48).

A popular part of this Sermon in Matthew promotes non-retaliation: "You have heard that it was said, 'An eye for an eye and a tooth for a tooth.' But I say to you, Do not resist one who is evil. But if any one strikes you on the right cheek, turn to him the other also" (Mt 5:38–39). Here Jesus is presented as quoting the Torah (Ex 21:24; Lev 24:20; Dt 19:21) and then goes beyond it with his "but I say to you." While Gandhi and many others believed this to be about violence, it appears to be more about insult, though it could easily extend to violence. How does one strike someone on the right cheek except by a backhanded slap which was insulting? Instead of escalating, Jesus is presented as advocating non-retaliation.

Non-retaliation was not unique to Matthew's Gospel. See Luke 6:29: "When reviled, we bless; when persecuted, we endure; when slandered, we try to conciliate" (also 1 Cor 4:12–13). Betz, in his *The Sermon on the Mount,* 288, quotes Cicero's *De Finibus*: "Right moreover, properly so styled and entitled, exists (they aver) by nature; and it is foreign to the nature of the Wise Man not only to do wrong but even to hurt anybody. Nor again is it righteous to enter into a partnership in wrongdoing with one's friends or benefactors" (288). John Meier agrees with Betz on non-retaliation in his *A Marginal Jew: Rethinking the Historical Jesus, Law and Love*, Vol. 4. where he writes, "the axiom on non-retaliation, the New Testament is inventing nothing" (542). Zerbe *in Non-retaliation in Early Jewish and New Testament Texts: Ethical Themes in Social Contexts* goes back to "The Counsels of Wisdom" (an Akkadian document from 700 BCE): "Do not return evil to the man who disputes you; Requite with kindness your evil doer. Maintain justice to your enemy. Smile on your adversary" (34). The Old Testament Book of Proverbs contains a number of non-retaliatory texts: "A person's wisdom yields patience; it is to one's glory to overlook an offense" (19:11). Later, in Proverbs 24:29, we read, "Do not say, 'As they did to me, so will I do to them; I will repay them according to their deeds'" (NAB). Kindness toward enemies follows in ch. 25: "If your enemies are hungry, give them food to eat, if thirsty, give something to drink; For live coals you will heap on their heads" (Prov. 25:21–22 NAB).

However widespread the teaching on non-retaliation, N.T. authors saw its importance especially among people following a leader who was in conflict with his religious tradition and the Temple state while they themselves were also in tension with both Roman and Herodian rule and parts of Jewish tradition.

The Sermon on the Mount continues in chapter 6 where Jesus takes standard modes of Jewish piety: alms giving, prayer, and fasting and gives critical correction by saying each of these practices ought to be done in secret in relation to God, not in order to gain human approval.

An important issue in chapter 6 is Jesus' advocacy of debt forgiveness in the Lord's Prayer (Mt 6:12), which is related to his opposition to mammon ("You cannot serve God and mammon," Mt 6:24). Mammon means stored money, not subsistence (Oakman 91). What was his problem with mammon? It was tied up with the oppressive regime of urban elites, Herodians, and Romans who were taxing peasants and forcing them into unending debt.

One difficulty in referring to Jesus as "teacher" is this title usually applies to his opponents in Matthew's Gospel, "teachers of the law." There are at least 14 references to "teachers of the law" in Matthew's Gospel including the reference to a passion prediction in which teachers of the law will condemn Jesus: "'We are going up to Jerusalem, and the Son of Man will be betrayed to the chief priests and the teachers of the law'" (Mt 20:18). There are, however, numerous instances where Jesus is directly addressed as "teacher" (8:19; 19:16; 22:16; 22:24). A socially challenging text warns disciples of Jesus against being called teacher: "Nor are you to be called 'teacher,' for you have one Teacher, the Christ" (23:10). Here Jesus is presented as accepting the title "Christ."

Christ, or Messiah, in Mark was not a title Jesus embraced with comfort. In Matthew's Gospel, on the other hand, Jesus is presented as the heir to David by trying (not with complete success) to link Jesus with David in the genealogy. The genealogy links King David to Joseph by marriage, not by blood (Mt 1:16). Jesus, however, is more than a son of David, hence Messiah; he is son of God. To that end Matthew presents Jesus as issuing from God, not from Joseph. Virgin conception trumps the Davidic bloodline. There appears to be no evidence establishing Mary as a member of the line of David (Brown, Raymond E., *The Birth of the Messiah*, 89, 287).

The hidden Jesus of Mark is instead welcomed in Matthew's Gospel from his birth by the "wise men" (2:11 onward). The disciples in Matthew, far from failing to understand who Jesus is, give him homage.

Jesus being worshiped or at least given homage by the disciples in Matthew versus not being understood by the disciples in Mark raises the question of which is more accurate. This question presumes the Gospels are similar to news accounts or historical accounts. While there is historical information in the Gospels, they are primarily conveying material to help people live a Christian life. Here Matthew appears to have considerable sense of freedom

Table 3.1. Mark 6:48-52 and Matthew 14:25–27, 32–33

Mark 6:48–52	Matthew 14:25–27, 32–33
About the fourth watch of the night he went out to them, walking on the lake. He was about to pass by them, ⁴⁹but when they saw him walking on the lake, they thought he was a ghost. They cried out, ⁵⁰because they all saw him and were terrified. Immediately he spoke to them and said, "Take courage! It is I. Don't be afraid." ⁵¹Then he climbed into the boat with them, and the wind died down. They were completely amazed, ⁵²for they had not understood about the loaves; their hearts were hardened.	²⁵During the fourth watch of the night Jesus went out to them, walking on the lake. ²⁶When the disciples saw him walking on the lake, they were terrified. "It's a ghost," they said, and cried out in fear. ²⁷But Jesus immediately said to them: "Take courage! It is I. Don't be afraid . . . " ³²And when they climbed into the boat, the wind died down. ³³Then those who were in the boat worshiped him, saying, "Truly you are the Son of God."

in altering the text he has received from Mark. (Why assume Mark is prior will be easier to answer when we come to the chapter on Luke.) Matthew is telling the story to make a different point from Mark; he is teaching another lesson. You may want to know what actually happened, but there are no more ancient and more reliable texts than the Gospels when one wants information about Jesus. Trying to get behind these texts to the historical material is usually marked with uncertainty. Here we will focus primarily on what the evangelists are attempting to communicate.

JESUS FOUNDER OF CHURCH AUTHORITY

Jesus is not only recognized and given homage by the disciples, but also their image is considerably improved in Matthew's Gospel. Matthew diminishes the ignorance of the disciples, which Mark was stressing. Why would Matthew do this?

Notice the differences in the following two versions of the same story:

Table 3.2. Mk 8:14-21 and Mt 16:5-12

Mk 8:14–21	Mt 16:5–12
¹⁴The disciples had forgotten to bring bread, except for one loaf they had with them in the boat. ¹⁵"Be careful," Jesus warned them. "Watch out for the yeast of the Pharisees and that of Herod." ¹⁶They discussed this with one another and said, "It is because we have no bread." ¹⁷Aware of their discussion, Jesus asked them: "Why are you talking about having no bread? Do you still not see or understand? *Are your hearts hardened?* ¹⁸*Do you have eyes but fail to see, and ears but fail to hear?* And don't you remember? ¹⁹When I broke the five loaves for the five thousand, how many basketfuls of pieces did you pick up?" "Twelve," they replied. ²⁰"And when I broke the seven loaves for the four thousand, how many basketfuls of pieces did you pick up?" They answered, "Seven." ²¹He said to them, *"Do you still not understand?"*	⁵When they went across the lake, the disciples forgot to take bread. ⁶"Be careful," Jesus said to them. "Be on your guard against the yeast of the Pharisees and Sadducees." ⁷They discussed this among themselves and said, "It is because we didn't bring any bread." ⁸Aware of their discussion, Jesus asked, "You of little faith, why are you talking among yourselves about having no bread? ⁹Do you still not understand? Don't you remember the five loaves for the five thousand, and how many basketfuls you gathered? ¹⁰Or the seven loaves for the four thousand, and how many basketfuls you gathered? ¹¹How is it you don't understand that I was not talking to you about bread? But be on your guard against the yeast of the Pharisees and Sadducees." ¹²*Then they understood* that he was not telling them to guard against the yeast used in bread, but against the teaching of the Pharisees and Sadducees.

Another example of improving the image of the disciples is in the transfiguration. In Mark 9, the disciples come down the mountain "questioning" without any indication of their understanding, whereas in Matthew the disciples "understood" (Mt 17:13).

The toning down of the disciples' ignorance serves Matthew's agenda of establishing church authority. In the four Gospels, only Matthew uses the word "church." He uses the word twice where he has Jesus establishing church authority in chapters 16 and 18.

In chapter 16, Jesus asks Peter who Peter and others say he is. In Mark, this immediately leads to passion prediction and misunderstanding. In Matthew, however, a section on church authority is added to what Matthew receives from Mark's text.

The argument with Peter occurs in both Mark in Matthew after this passage, but in Matthew Peter has authorization by Jesus.

In Matthew 18, on community regulations, we have a passage on regulations unique to Matthew that endows the disciples with credibility and respectability as they are given the mission to mediate and judge serious moral issues. What should the community do with a member who is sinning and recalcitrant?

The closest parallel is Luke 17:3, which says nothing about church authority nor about treating the stubbornly disobedient sinner as "a pagan" or better as "a Gentile" (The Greek for this is εθνικος, *ethnikos*, from which the English word "ethnic" gives the meaning of "people," the other peoples of the world aside from the Jews.) or a" tax collector." This emphasis on church

Table 3.3. Mark 9:9-13 and Mt 17:9-13

Mark 9:9–13	Mt 17:9–13
[9]And as they were coming down the mountain, he charged them to tell no one what they had seen, until the Son of man should have risen from the dead. [10]So they kept the matter to themselves, *questioning* what the rising from the dead meant. [11]And they asked him, "Why do the scribes say that first Elijah must come?" [12]And he said to them, "Elijah does come first to restore all things; and how is it written of the Son of man, that he should suffer many things and be treated with contempt? [13]But I tell you that Elijah has come, and they did to him whatever they pleased, as it is written of him."	And as they were coming down the mountain, Jesus commanded them, "Tell no one the vision, until the Son of man is raised from the dead." [10]And the disciples asked him, "Then why do the scribes say that first Elijah must come?" [11]He replied, "Elijah does come, and he is to restore all things; [12]but I tell you that Elijah has already come, and they did not know him, but did to him whatever they pleased. So also the Son of man will suffer at their hands." [13]Then *the disciples understood* that he was speaking to them of John the Baptist.

Table 3.4. Mark 8:27-31 and Matthew 16:13-21

Mark 8:27–31	Matthew 16:13–21
[27]Jesus and his disciples went on to the villages around Caesarea Philippi. On the way he asked them, "Who do people say I am?" [28]They replied, "Some say John the Baptist; others say Eliah; and still others, one of the prophets." [29]"But what about you?" he asked. "Who do you say I am?" Peter answered, "You are the Christ." [30]Jesus warned them not to tell anyone about him. [31]He then began to teach them that the Son of Man must suffer many things and be rejected by the elders, chief priests and teachers of the law, and that he must be killed and after three days rise again.	[13]When Jesus came to the region of Caesarea Philippi, he asked his disciples, "Who do people say the Son of Man is?" [14]They replied, "Some say John the Baptist; others say Elijah; and still others, Jeremiah or one of the prophets." [15]"But what about you?" he asked. "Who do you say I am?" [16]Simon Peter answered, "You are the Christ, the Son of the living God." [17]Jesus replied, "Blessed are you, Simon son of Jonah, for this was not revealed to you by man, but by my Father in heaven. [18]And I tell you that you are Peter, and on this rock I will build my church, and the gates of Hades will not overcome it. [19]I will give you the keys of the kingdom of heaven; whatever you bind on earth will be bound in heaven, and whatever you loose on earth will be loosed in heaven." [20]Then he warned his disciples not to tell anyone that he was the Christ. [21]From that time on Jesus began to explain to his disciples that he must go to Jerusalem and suffer many things at the hands of the elders, chief priests and teachers of the law, and that he must be killed and on the third day be raised to life.

authority is situated along with a statement that cannot easily be reconciled with what the Gospels suggest about Jesus. Would Jesus use this phrase "Gentile or tax collector" as title for a category of the stubbornly disobedient? Elsewhere in Matthew's Gospel (9:9; 10:3), Jesus calls and accepts tax collectors into his intimate band of disciples. The prejudice against tax collectors would be reinforced by this saying in Mt 18:17.

In Matthew's Gospel this stereotypical way of thinking concerning tax collectors shows up one other time: "If you love those who love you, what reward will you get? Are not even the tax collectors doing that?" (Mt 5:46). Do these texts suggest Jesus had a prejudice against tax collectors or perhaps the author of Matthew's Gospel did? If one opts to believe the text came from Jesus, then Jesus is founding the church and has a problem with tax collectors. An alternative would be the author of Matthew's Gospel is establishing

Table 3.5. Matthew 18:15-18 and Luke 17:3

Matthew 18:15–18	*Luke 17:3*
[15]"If your brother sins against you, go and show him his fault, just between the two of you. If he listens to you, you have won your brother over. [16]But if he will not listen, take one or two others along, so that 'every matter may be established by the testimony of two or three witnesses.' [17]If he refuses to listen to them, tell it to the church; and if he refuses to listen even to the church, treat him as you would a pagan or a tax collector. [18]"I tell you the truth, whatever you bind on earth will be bound in heaven, and whatever you loose on earth will be loosed in heaven."	[3]So watch yourselves. "If your brother sins, rebuke him, and if he repents, forgive him."

church authority as the Christian community was maturing and having to deal with moral issues and the behavior of its members.

The same analysis would apply to "Gentiles." Did Jesus have a bias against Gentiles that he was overcoming or is this an expression of the author of Matthew's gospel (see Mt 5:47; 6:7; 6:32; 18:17)? These utterances occur in Matthew exclusively except for once in Luke: "And do not seek what you are to eat and what you are to drink, nor be of anxious mind. For all the nations [*ethne* = Gentiles] of the world seek these things; and your Father knows that you need them" (Lk 12:29–30 RSV). The author uses anti-Gentile stereotypes which would appeal to a Jewish audience.

It would be easier to ascribe this sort of language to Jesus, if multiple sources would attest to it and if it did not conflict with his more welcoming statements toward tax collectors and pagans/Gentiles. The search for the likely statements of the historical Jesus is generally tentative, but the criteria of coherence with other statements attributed to Jesus and multiple attestation do not give much support to this coming from Jesus. In this book we are concerned not so much the historical Jesus as the intention of the authors. Matthew presents Jesus as the one who establishes church authority. The diminished ignorance of the disciples in Matthew's Gospel helps to establish them as worthy recipients of Jesus' approbation.

DEATH OF JESUS AS FULFILLMENT OF JEWISH HOPE

The dominant element in the Matthean portrayal of Jesus is as fulfillment of Jewish hope. A final focal point for this is the death of Jesus. In Mark's Gospel, the death of Jesus was the dramatic moment of recognition by the centurion. This summarizes the entire movement of Mark from lack of human recognition to acknowledgement at the foot of the cross. The death of Jesus in Matthew functions in a similarly summary fashion.

The most remarkable difference between Mark's death scene and Matthew's rendering is the impact of the death. In both Mark and Matthew, the curtain of the Temple is torn in two at the death of Jesus, which is a comment on the end of the Temple prepared for by Jesus' conflict with the Temple (Mk 11:11,15–17; Mt 21:10–17). The cursing and death of the fig tree are symbolic of the barrenness and consequent destruction of Jerusalem (Mk 11:12–14; Mt 21:18–19). What Matthew adds is an earthquake and tombs opening with people coming out of the tombs and appearing to many people. After this, the centurion and those with him declare Jesus to be son of God.

> At that moment the curtain of the Temple was torn in two from top to bottom. The earth shook and the rocks split. The tombs broke open and the bodies of many holy people who had died were raised to life. They came out of the tombs, and after Jesus' resurrection they went into the holy city and appeared to many people.
>
> When the centurion and those with him who were guarding Jesus saw the earthquake and all that had happened, they were terrified, and exclaimed, "Surely he was the Son of God!" (Matthew 27:51–54)

The splitting of rocks has biblical associations with the presence and action of God. "He shakes the earth from its place . . . " (Job 9:6; see also Judges 5:4; 2 Sm 22:8; Psalms 78:15; 104:32; Senior, 313).

Aside from the awesome display of power, the imagery of tombs opening inserts the death of Jesus into an apocalyptic drama. Historically minded students often ask how Mark could miss this bizarre event. It is not likely that what would have been one of the most amazing events in world history would be ignored by the other evangelists. It is not difficult, however, to figure out how the scene is functioning in Matthew's passion narrative.

The Hebrew Bible gives a parallel to the opening of tombs in Ezekiel 37. There the scene was to provide hope to disillusioned Jews who had been taken into exile in Babylonia. The people of Judah of the southern kingdom were taken away from their promised land. Ezekiel goes on to speak of a united kingdom that will be restored in the land of Israel. The scene depicts dry bones; the Hebrew people were promised a land flowing with milk and honey, but there they are dying off in a foreign land. What happened to God's promises?

> Then he said to me: "Son of man, these bones are the whole house of Israel. They say, 'Our bones are dried up and our hope is gone; we are cut off.' Therefore prophesy and say to them: 'This is what the Sovereign LORD says: O my people, I am going to open your graves and bring you up from them; I will bring you back to the land of Israel. Then you, my people, will know that I am the LORD, when I open your graves and bring you up from them. I will put my Spirit in you and you will live, and I will settle you in your own land. Then you will know that I the LORD have spoken, and I have done it, declares the LORD.' . . . This is what the Sovereign LORD says: 'Iwill take the Israelites out of the nations where they have gone. I will gather them from all around and bring them back into their own land. I will make them one nation in the land, on the mountains of Israel. There will be one king over all of them and they will never again be two nations or be divided into two kingdoms.'" (Ezk 37:11–14; 21–22)

"I will open your graves and bring you up from them; I will bring you back to the land of Israel" (Ezk. 37:13) is a text that Matthew uses to give meaning to the resurrection of Jesus as a fulfillment of Jewish hope.

This text was precious to Israel and was used in a setting contemporary to Matthew by Jewish zealots who were resisting Roman rule. With the destruction of the Temple by Romans some Jewish resistors hid themselves on the top of the mountain known as Masada in the Judean desert. Josephus, the Jewish historian in his *Wars of the Jews* written around 75 CE, describes the fortress and the events: "There was a fortress of very great strength not far from Jerusalem, which had been built by our ancient kings. . . . It was called Masada" (*Wars of the Jews,* 4.7.2). Herod the Great had used Masada to protect his family against his enemies. On the top of this mountain, there were buildings and cisterns that could support life indefinitely. With Jewish resistance fighters on the mountain, Roman troops surrounded Masada and constructed a ramp out of stones and earth that would enable them to storm the people finding refuge there. Today after 2000 years, one may see remnants of these military encampments on the desert floor from the top of Masada, and the ramp is still largely intact. According to Josephus, the Jewish resisters decided to commit suicide rather than submit to Roman slavery or death.

> They then chose ten men by lot out of them to slay all the rest; every one of whom laid himself down by his wife and children on the ground, and threw his arms about them, and they offered their necks to the stroke of those who by lot executed that melancholy office; and when these ten had, without fear, slain them all, they made the same rule for casting lots for themselves, that he

whose lot it was should first kill the other nine, and after all should kill himself. Accordingly, all these had courage sufficient to be no way behind one another in doing or suffering; so, for a conclusion, the nine offered their necks to the executioner, and he who was the last of all took a view of all the other bodies, lest perchance some or other among so many that were slain should want his assistance to be quite despatched, and when he perceived that they were all slain, he set fire to the palace, and with the great force of his hand ran his sword entirely through himself, and fell down dead near to his own relations. So these people died with this intention, that they would not leave so much as one soul among them all alive to be subject to the Romans. Yet was there an ancient woman, and another who was of kin to Eleazar, and superior to most women in prudence and learning, with five children, who had concealed themselves in caverns underground, and had carried water thither for their drink, and were hidden there when the rest were intent upon the slaughter of one another. Those others were nine hundred and sixty in number, the women and children being withal included in that computation. This calamitous slaughter was made on the fifteenth day of the month Xanthicus [Nisan]. (Josephus, *Wars of the Jews*, 7.9.1)

The text of Josephus may contain embellishment to create a kind of heroic story of Jewish resistance (see Ben-Yehuda). Notice even Josephus speaks of "slaughter"; all may not have been eager to die. The need for exhortation by their leader suggests reluctance to die, though he reports eventual willingness after exhortations. Yigdael Yadin, in the 1960s, helped to excavate the synagogue in Masada and had found fragments of Ezekiel 37 there (Yadin, 187). The Jews who watched day after day the approaching Roman soldiers found hope in the text of Ezekiel that God would bring life out of death, the same text that gave hope to the Hebrew people in exile. Matthew uses this sacred text to say God will bring life out of death, beginning with the resurrection of Jesus. As demonstrated in this chapter, fulfillment of Jewish hope is a dominant theme in the portrayal of Jesus by Matthew's Gospel.

Notwithstanding the prominence of the element of fulfillment, another overarching theme finds strong development in Matthew's Gospel, namely the kingdom of God. Many regard this as the central preaching of Jesus, and it cuts across the boundaries of the first three gospels. I will introduce it here as Matthew adds an entire chapter (13) of parables to the smaller Gospel of Mark. (We will return to topic of kingdom of God back in discussion of Luke's Gospel where there are parables challenging conventional thinking.)

PREACHER OF KINGDOM OF GOD

Parables are extended metaphors or similes. When Jesus used the notion of kingdom or rule of God, it already had a history which would have influenced the way it was understood.

In the Jewish groups contemporaneous to Jesus or the New Testament, the zealots would have had the simplest concept. For them God's rule would be established by overthrowing the Romans and those who cooperated with the Romans; Jewish self-rule would be God's rule (see Josephus, *Wars*, 4). Violent revolution would be the way to establish God's kingdom. The Pharisees would hasten the coming of kingdom through strict observance of law. Jesus who broke some Sabbath laws did not share their perspective. The Sadducees who ran the Temple would have had an overriding concern with ritual. That Jesus compared the kingdom of heaven with leaven would not have endeared him to them; leavened bread was forbidden from Temple ritual as it was a sign of corruption. The Essenes would have had difficulty with Jesus' message as he did not live apart as they did (Philo, *Hypothetica*, 11.1).

The New Testament does not give a definition of the kingdom of God; examination of parables will help us to clarify what Jesus meant by this concept which appears to be at odds with the understanding of his contemporaries.

Crossan in his book *In Parables* organizes the parables into three categories based on his analysis of the parable of the treasure in a field: parables of advent, of reversal and of action. "The kingdom of heaven is like treasure hidden in a field. When a man found it, he hid it again, and then in his joy went and sold all he had and bought that field" (Mt 13:44).

This parable gives a scene with surprise and joyful discovery of something hidden; Crossan sees this as typical of the kingdom. The type of parable that focuses on this element of God's ruling power he calls parables of advent. The second characteristic of this parable is reversal; the man sold all that he had. This implies a reversal of values or direction. This is the element that Luke develops and will be treated in that chapter. The third characteristic of this parable which Crossan uses to categorize parables is the buying of the field which he sees as typifying parables of action. The ruling power of God is something mysterious, not on the surface which when encountered brings joy and a major change in values or direction in life and finally decisive action (Crossan 37+).

Parables of the coming of the Kingdom involve hiddenness, surprise, unexpectedness, joyful discovery. In Matthew 13:33, the woman hides the leaven or yeast in the dough. The Greek word is *enekrypsen*, ενεκρυψεν, forms of which are used twice in 13:44 when referring to the hidden treasure. This verb is related to the English word "to encrypt." When making dough the yeast is no longer seen, but one can see its effects; the power of God is present but not obvious.

In 13:31, the parable of the mustard seed involves a small seed when planted but large when grown, an unexpected growth. In the parable of the mustard seed, there is the contrast between the smallness of the seed and the largeness of the plant. Despite the smallness of the seed, the large shrub grows. God's power is unexpected (13:31–32).

In the parable of the sower (13:3+), there is a contrast between losses and gains. In spite of the three examples of losses along the path, on rocky ground, on thorns there are three examples of abundance: hundredfold, sixtyfold, and thirtyfold. Despite these losses, there are abundant yields. The kingdom of God challenges ordinary expectation (Crossan 41+).

The parables of the yeast hidden in dough and the unexpected growth from mustard seed, lend themselves to a political interpretation if one takes Jesus' historical context seriously. He was talking to peasants for whom the obvious authoritative words about God came from the religious elite and the corrupt administration who were exploiting these people. By emphasizing the hidden and the unexpected, Jesus is cautioning his hearers to be skeptical towards the professional interpreters of God. He is saying if you assume that God's rule is invested with the professional religious who are running the Temple, think again! The parable of seed falling on bad soil and finally on good soil makes special sense to people whose history has involved repeated conquest by foreign powers and who now are suffering under the rule of the Temple state. Despite the numerous losses (bad soil) there will be restoration (abundance). Jesus is offering hope to his fellow peasants; the kingdom of heaven is theirs: "Blessed are the poor in spirit, for theirs is the kingdom of heaven. Blessed are those who mourn, for they shall be comforted. Blessed are the meek, for they shall inherit the earth. Blessed are those who hunger and thirst for righteousness, for they shall be satisfied" (Mt 5:3–6).

Not all parables easily admit to a political interpretation. There are several parables which convey hope besides the above mentioned abundant harvest (13:3+), hidden Divine influence (yeast 13:44), namely lost sheep (Mt 18:12–14), hidden treasure (13:44), and pearl of great price (13:45).

Matthew portrays Jesus as one fulfilling Jewish hope through using prophecies. While his use of prophecy is sometimes forced, hope nevertheless finds expression in Jesus' preaching both in the Sermon on the Mount through beatitudes (5:3–12) and in his characterization of God's indiscriminate love (5:45) and providential care (6:26–32) as well as in several parables.

Chapter 4

Luke

Jesus as Martyr Prophet, Champion of the Poor, Model of Prayer, Innocent and Merciful Savior

Key questions to pose of the text of Luke's Gospel:

1. Find the Lucan equivalent to Matthew 5:48 in Luke 6.
2. Contrast Mark 6:4 and Luke 4:24; explain the difference.
3. Contrast Mark 3:31 with Luke 8:19–20; explain the difference.
4. Contrast Mark 14:3–4 with Luke 7:36–50.
5. From where in the Old Testament does the reference to casting fire come in Luke 9:54?

Discussion questions:

1. What in the parable of banquet guests in Luke 14 might be challenging to contemporary Christians?
2. What in the series of woes in Luke 6 would be difficult for contemporary Christians to hear?

Luke presents expansion of Christianity throughout the Roman empire in his Gospel and Acts of the Apostles. For Luke, Jesus is a sympathetic figure, a merciful and innocent martyr thereby encouraging his followers to live peacefully under Roman rule while maintaining their own values. Jesus is presented with prominent concern for the poor.

The author of Luke's Gospel and Acts of the Apostles projects Christianity as a world- wide movement co-extensive with the Roman Empire. This can be seen in his geographical structure: In Acts he moves the focus progressively further away from Jerusalem to the political capital of the world, Rome (Acts 28). Luke thus presents Roman officials in a relatively positive way, for example Pilate and Herod find Jesus innocent: see Luke 23 where Jesus is repeatedly declared innocent by the Roman official Pilate, but the Jewish crowd wants him to be crucified.

Pilate in Mark "wondered" and asked why he should be killed. Instead, Pilate in Luke again and again declares Jesus innocent. Notice in Acts 25:24–25, the friendly relationships with Roman officials. The persecution of Jesus is paralleled with the persecution of Paul, and both presentations of persecution contain the relative benevolence of the Romans.

> Brethren, though I [Paul] had done nothing against the people or the customs of our fathers, yet I was delivered prisoner from Jerusalem into the hands of the Romans. When they had examined me, they wished to set me at liberty, because there was no reason for the death penalty in my case. But when the Jews objected, I was compelled to appeal to Caesar. (Acts 28:17–19)

Early in Luke's Gospel, Mary and Joseph are shown to be cooperative with the Roman census (Luke 2:1–2) which Jews did not generally accept (Acts 5:37; 1 Chron. 21:1). These elements suggest to the reader living under Roman rule that Christianity is compatible with life under Roman administration. Christians can live out their faith without having to attack the Romans. The execution of Jesus by the Romans, on the other hand, would suggest to some, that Christians would be enemies of the Romans. Luke wants to downplay the enmity between the Romans and Christians to protect Christians from Roman persecution. Another example shows up where Luke somewhat depoliticizes the entrance of Jesus to Jerusalem by inserting "peace in heaven" (ch. 19:38). Heavenly order is no threat to Roman regime. Luke wants Christians to live in harmony with Roman rule.

With Luke's view that the Spirit of God will work through Christian churches as they spread throughout the Roman empire, he does not completely endorse a notion of an immediate end to history or the world: "He proceeded to tell a parable, because he was near to Jerusalem, and because they supposed that the kingdom of God was to appear immediately." This appears only in Luke 19:11–12. (He nevertheless keeps "this generation" 21:32.)

Luke, in Acts, blames Jews numerous times for the death of Jesus. We could speculate why. Romans, by the time of writing Luke's Gospel and Acts had combatted Jewish rebellions, and the Temple has been destroyed. ("Your enemies will cast up a bank about you and surround you," 19:43. "But when you see Jerusalem surrounded by armies, then know that its desolation has come near," 21:20+.)

To promote harmony with the Romans, the author of Acts would like to affect the perception of Christians by putting distance between Christians and the Jews who did not accept Jesus. The "Jews" according to Luke's Gospel are prone to mob rule: "Away with this man, and release to us Barabbas" (23:18). The violence of the Roman official is downplayed, while the Jewish mob cries out to kill Jesus. Luke in Acts also uses this Roman stereotype of the Jews as troublesome, especially in Acts of the Apostles thus distinguishing from and opposing Christians to Jews. The Roman historian Tacitus, for example writes about Jews:

> All their other customs, which are at once perverse and disgusting, owe their strength to their very badness. The most degraded out of other races, scorning their national beliefs, brought to them their contributions and presents. This augmented the wealth of the Jews, as also did the fact, that among themselves they are inflexibly honest and ever ready to shew compassion, though they regard the rest of mankind with all the hatred of enemies. They sit apart at meals, they sleep apart, and though, as a nation, they are singularly prone to lust, they abstain from intercourse with foreign women; among themselves nothing is unlawful. Circumcision was adopted by them as a mark of difference from other men. Those who come over to their religion adopt the practice, and have this lesson first instilled into them, to despise all gods, to disown their country, and set at nought parents, children, and brethren. (*Histories*, Book 5 [c. 109 CE])

In 120 CE, Suetonius reports about Emperor Claudius who "expelled from Rome Jews who were making constant disturbances at the instigation of Chrestus" (*Life of Claudius*, 25.4).

These apparent troublemakers according to Luke's Gospel and Acts of the Apostles are responsible for the death of Jesus, despite crucifixion being a Roman act.

> And they began to accuse him, saying, "We found this man perverting our nation, and forbidding us to give tribute to Caesar, and saying that he himself is Christ a king." (Lk 23:2)

> But they were urgent, saying, "He stirs up the people." (Lk 23:5)

> The chief priests and the scribes stood by, vehemently accusing him. (Lk 23:10)

> But they all cried out together, "Away with this man." (Lk 23:18)

> But they shouted out, "Crucify, crucify him!" (Lk 23:21)

> "But they were urgent, demanding with loud cries that he should be crucified. And their voices prevailed." (Lk 23:23)

This Jesus. . . . You crucified and killed. (Acts 2:22–23)

This Jesus . . . whom you crucified. (Acts. 2:36)

You . . . killed the Author of life. (Acts 3:12–15a)

By the name of Jesus . . . whom you crucified. (Acts 4:8b–10)

Jesus . . . whom you killed by hanging him. (Acts 5:30)

The righteous one whom you have now betrayed and murdered. (Acts 7:51–52)

They put him to death by hanging him on a tree. (Acts 10:39)

They asked Pilate to have him killed. (Acts 13:27–28)

Luke also blames Jews for the persecution of Paul: "But the Jews incited the devout women of high standing and the leading men of the city, and stirred up persecution against Paul" (Acts 13:50).

This distancing of Jesus and Christianity from the Jews, at least from the Jews who did not accept Jesus, furthers the author's mission to show Christianity as compatible with Roman rule. While some Romans distinguished between Christians and Jews, not all did. Some Romans would not have separated out Christians and Jews, and many Christians would have seen themselves as Jewish in the early days (Acts 2:46; 3:1; 18:2, 26). Romans described both Christians and Jews as practicing superstition (Tacitus, *Annals*, 15; Cicero in "Pro Flaccus," 28), as well as hating humankind (Tacitus, *Histories*, 5, and *Annals*, 15). When Acts of the Apostles declares "Jews" being expelled, that included Jewish Christians: "After this, Paul left Athens and went to Corinth. There he met a Jew named Aquila, a native of Pontus, who had recently come from Italy with his wife Priscilla, because Claudius had ordered all Jews to leave Rome" (Acts 18:2).

Understanding the use of stereotypical thinking in relation to Jews as part of Luke's historical situation of trying to protect Christians from Roman persecution could help to prevent contemporary readers from universalizing negative attributions to Jews. Even if Jesus challenged some of the power brokers of his day, he could not legitimately be accused of being anti-Jewish.

Luke offers an alternative to Roman values. Despite the relatively positive image given to Roman authorities in Luke/Acts the author is promoting an alternative to Roman authority. While not advocating overthrow of Roman rule, the author is putting forth the idea of the Christian movement as restoring God's rule: "For mine eyes have seen thy salvation which thou hast prepared in the presence of all peoples, a light for revelation to the Gentiles, and for glory to thy people Israel" (Luke 2:30–32).

In short, the Christian movement envisioned by Luke is not anti-state, nor does it target Rome for violent revolution, but rather by embracing a different set of values, the Christian movement under its Lord will transform life under Roman rule. The mighty will be put down; the lowly raised up (Lk 1). Christians will not be slaves of wealth, power, honor, and status.

And he lifted up his eyes on his disciples and said:

Blessed are you poor, for yours is the kingdom of God.

Blessed are you that hunger now, for you shall be satisfied.

Blessed are you that weep now, for you shall laugh.

Blessed are you when men hate you, and when they exclude you and revile you, and cast out your name as evil, on account of the Son of man! Rejoice in that day, and leap for joy, for behold, your reward is great in heaven; for so their fathers did to the prophets.

But woe to you that are rich, for you have received your consolation.

Woe to you that are full now, for you shall hunger.

Woe to you that laugh now, for you shall mourn and weep.

Woe to you, when all men speak well of you, for so their fathers did to the false prophets. (Lk 6:20–26)

It is not easy to characterize the values of the Roman empire fairly but here are a few points of contrast; Christians would not engage in emperor worship.

Christians were not fans of violence which contrasts with Roman love of violence in gladiatorial spectacles, to say nothing of their ongoing worldwide military conquests.

Christians would have had difficulty reconciling Jesus' mercy toward adulterers in John 8 and the Julian marriage law (#123) which allowed a father to kill his daughter caught in adultery.

Augustus supported and promoted hierarchical ranks, not role reversal, for example Suetonius writes of seating discrimination in theatres:

Whenever any public show was given anywhere, the first row of seats should be reserved for senators; and at Rome he would not allow the envoys of the free and allied nations to sit in the orchestra, since he was informed that even freedmen were sometimes appointed. He separated the soldiery from the people. 2 He assigned special seats to the married men of the commons. (Suetonius, "The Life of Augustus," 44)

Hierarchical discrimination does not fit early Christian ideas about putting down the mighty and raising up the lowly (Lk 1:52) or having all things in common (Acts 4:32–34).

Luke's softening of Jesus' political stance in relation to Rome is best understood in Luke's historical moment. Early followers had expected Jesus to liberate them from the Romans: "But we had hoped that he was the one to redeem Israel" (Lk 24:21). In spite of this disappointment over Jesus' failure to oust the Romans, Jesus is presented as a savior. While that salvation is connected with the need to protect Christians from Roman values, it extends to their relationship with God.

Of this man's [David] posterity God has brought to Israel a Savior, Jesus, as he promised. . . . Let it be known to you therefore, brethren, that through this man forgiveness of sins is proclaimed to you, and by him every one that believes is freed from everything from which you could not be freed by the law of Moses. (Acts 13:23, 38–39)

Despite the political softening in regard to Roman rule, challenges to conventional values and assumptions can be found in every chapter of Luke's Gospel. Christians could live under Roman rule, but they are called to question and change. More on the challenges to conventional thinking in the following sections.

PROPHET

The usual definition of a prophet that I hear in a classroom from students is someone who can predict the future. This is not central to the meaning of a biblical prophet. Predicting the future crept into Hebrew prophecy thanks to Greek culture where oracles were respected. More predominant to biblical prophets is the idea that they have a keen insight into what God wants to communicate to a community, and they deliver God's message (see Jer 7:1–20).

Table 4.1. Mark 6:4 and Luke 4:24

Mark 6:4	Luke 4:24
"Jesus said to them, 'Only in his hometown, among his relatives and in his own house is a prophet without honor.'"	"'I tell you the truth,' he continued, 'no prophet is accepted in his hometown.'"

Multiple times, Luke's Gospel identifies Jesus as a prophet. One can locate references to Jesus as prophet in Mark and Matthew as well, but Luke develops this more than they. A passage in Mark with its parallel in Luke will help us with the question of the priority of Mark.

In Mark's Gospel, with its emphasis on the misunderstanding of Jesus, we see him as a dishonored prophet in his own house, among his relatives, and in his hometown or native place. In Luke's version of this saying, the people who do not honor Jesus are those in his hometown. The references to the family of Jesus are eliminated from among those who do not accept him. Why does Luke change this, and why assume that Luke follows Mark rather than the other way around?

Luke's Gospel begins with an infancy narrative in which Mary, the mother of Jesus, is told by the angel Gabriel the identity of her son. With this knowledge, for the sake of consistency at least, she cannot later dishonor him. Furthermore, Luke apparently has information about Mary as praying with the apostles after the resurrection, and this appreciation of Mary helps to shape his presentation of Mary. "They all joined together constantly in prayer, along with the women and Mary the mother of Jesus, and with his brothers" (Acts 1:14).

The repairing of the image of Mary also shows up in chapter 8.

The passage in Mark 3 contains a contrast between those inside the house who sat around Jesus who do God's will and those outside, his blood family. In Luke's version the contrast is eliminated, and Mary is included among those who hear and live out God's word.

If one did not assume Mark's Gospel as prior to Luke, one would have to believe Mark would consciously deny the close association with the apostles

Table 4.2. Mark 3:31–35 and Luke 8:18–21

Mark 3:31–35	Luke 8:18–21
[31]"Then Jesus' mother and brothers arrived. Standing outside, they sent someone in to call him. [32]A crowd was sitting around him, and they told him, 'Your mother and brothers are outside looking for you.'" [33]"'Who are my mother and my brothers?' he asked." [34]"Then he looked at those seated in a circle around him and said, 'Here are my mother and my brothers! [35]Whoever does God's will is my brother and sister and mother.'"	[18]"'Therefore consider carefully how you listen. Whoever has will be given more; whoever does not have, even what he thinks he has will be taken from him.'" [19]"Now Jesus' mother and brothers came to see him, but they were not able to get near him because of the crowd. [20]Someone told him, "'Your mother and brothers are standing outside, wanting to see you.'" [21]"He replied, 'My mother and brothers are those who hear God's word and put it into practice.'"

(Acts 1:14), her knowledge of who Jesus is (infancy narrative), and her being included among those who hear and do the word of God (Lk 8:18–21). This conscious denial would not be easy for Mark however much he wanted to stress the lack of understanding Jesus encountered. The priority of Mark hypothesis, on the other hand, would merely involve his narrative with his apparent lack of knowledge of the place of Mary in the early church, and lack of any infancy narrative as opposed to conscious denials (for more on the priority Mark see Brown, *Introduction to the New Testament*, 165).

While Jesus is mentioned as a prophet in Mark, Luke develops the theme. He is called a prophet by others: "A great prophet has risen among us" (7:16), "if this man were a prophet" (7:39). On the road to Emmaus, one of his disciples tells the not yet recognized risen Christ, "He was a prophet, powerful in word and deed before God and all the people" (24:19). These passages relate to other dimensions of Jesus as prophet.

Luke's Gospel is the most prophetic of the Gospels as it is filled with challenges to conventional thinking and acting. This supports the idea that Luke wanted to promote Christian values despite Roman rule. Since many of these challenges are found elsewhere in the Synoptic Gospels (e.g., Mt 15; Mk7; Mt 19:16+; Mk 10:17+; too many to cite), one may assume Jesus was behind the prophetic thrust of these sayings and stories. One will find prophetic challenges in nearly every chapter of Luke's Gospel; here are a few samples:

In chapter 1, the values of power and wealth come under attack: "He has put down the mighty from their thrones, and exalted those of low degree; he has filled the hungry with good things, and the rich he has sent empty away" (1:52–53).

Chapter 2 includes prophetic utterance concerning Jesus as source of division:

> Behold, this child is set for the fall and rising of many in Israel, and for a sign that is spoken against (and a sword will pierce through your own soul also), that thoughts out of many hearts may be revealed. (2:34–35)

Chapter 4 includes Jesus' temptation challenges the allure of political power:

> And the devil took him up, and showed him all the kingdoms of the world in a moment of time, ⁶and said to him, "To you I will give all this authority and their glory; for it has been delivered to me, and I give it to whom I will. ⁷If you, then, will worship me, it shall all be yours."⁸ And Jesus answered him, "It is written, 'You shall worship the Lord your God, and him only shall you serve.'" (4:4–8)

Jesus' prophetic challenge to people to widen their realm of concern is met with resistance:

The Spirit of the Lord is upon me,

because he has anointed me to preach good news to the poor.

He has sent me to proclaim release to the captives

and recovering of sight to the blind,

to set at liberty those who are oppressed,

to proclaim the acceptable year of the Lord.

And he closed the book, and gave it back to the attendant, and sat down; and the eyes of all in the synagogue were fixed on him. And he began to say to them, "Today this scripture has been fulfilled in your hearing." And all spoke well of him, and wondered at the gracious words which proceeded out of his mouth; and they said, "Is not this Joseph's son?" And he said to them, "Doubtless you will quote to me this proverb, 'Physician, heal yourself; what we have heard you did at Capernaum, do here also in your own country.'" And he said, "Truly, I say to you, no prophet is acceptable in his own country." (Lk 4:18–24)

In chapter 5, Jesus calls out prejudices surrounding lepers and tax collectors and sinners:

And the Pharisees and their scribes murmured against his disciples, saying, "Why do you eat and drink with tax collectors and sinners?" And Jesus answered them, "Those who are well have no need of a physician, but those who are sick; I have not come to call the righteous, but sinners to repentance." (5:30–32)

As in Mark's Gospel, he questions the importance of Sabbath law in relation to healing in chapter 6:

And Jesus said to them, "I ask you, is it lawful on the Sabbath to do good or to do harm, to save life or to destroy it?" And he looked around on them all, and said to him, "Stretch out your hand." And he did so, and his hand was restored. But they were filled with fury.

The sermon in chapter 6 aims to help people to move beyond retaliation and to affirm one's enemies:

> But I say to you that hear, Love your enemies, do good to those who hate you, bless those who curse you, pray for those who abuse you. To him who strikes you on the cheek, offer the other also; and from him who takes away your coat do not withhold even your shirt. (Lk 6:27–29)

Further in the sermon is the discrediting of defensive projection:

> Why do you see the speck that is in your brother's eye, but do not notice the log that is in your own eye? Or how can you say to your brother, "Brother, let me take out the speck that is in your eye," when you yourself do not see the log that is in your own eye? You hypocrite, first take the log out of your own eye, and then you will see clearly to take out the speck that is in your brother's eye. (6:41–42)

Luke chapter 7 has the story of a sinful woman who is praised and forgiven by Jesus over against a Pharisee: "You did not anoint my head with oil, but she has anointed my feet with ointment" (7:36–50).

Chapter 8 has Jesus reaching beyond the concern over ritual purity and impurity associated with bodily fluid:

> And a woman who had had a flow of blood for twelve years and could not be healed by any one, came up behind him, and touched the fringe of his garment; and immediately her flow of blood ceased. And Jesus said, "Who was it that touched me?" When all denied it, Peter said, "Master, the multitudes surround you and press upon you!" But Jesus said, "Someone touched me; for I perceive that power has gone forth from me." And when the woman saw that she was not hidden, she came trembling, and falling down before him declared in the presence of all the people why she had touched him, and how she had been immediately healed. And he said to her, "Daughter, your faith has made you well; go in peace." (8:43–48)

In chapter 9, Jesus confronts assumptions about the place of one's family in a disciple's life:

> As they were going along the road, a man said to him, "I will follow you wherever you go." And Jesus said to him, "Foxes have holes, and birds of the air have nests; but the Son of man has nowhere to lay his head." To another he said, "Follow me." But he said, "Lord, let me first go and bury my father." But he said to him, "Leave the dead to bury their own dead; but as for you, go and proclaim the kingdom of God." (9:57–60)

In both chapters 13 and 14, Jesus again challenges a myopic application of Sabbath law in favor of compassion:

But the ruler of the synagogue, indignant because Jesus had healed on the Sabbath, said to the people, "There are six days on which work ought to be done; come on those days and be healed, and not on the Sabbath day." Then the Lord answered him, "You hypocrites! Does not each of you on the Sabbath untie his ox or his ass from the manger, and lead it away to water it? And ought not this woman, a daughter of Abraham whom Satan bound for eighteen years, be loosed from this bond on the Sabbath day?" (13:4–16)

And Jesus spoke to the lawyers and Pharisees, saying, "Is it lawful to heal on the Sabbath, or not?" (14:3)

Chapter 19 presents Jesus offering salvation to a rich tax collector: "And when they saw it they all murmured, 'He has gone in to be the guest of a man who is a sinner'" (19:7).

Chapter 21 challenges the belief in the stability of life symbolized by the massive size of the Temple: "And as some spoke of the temple, how it was adorned with noble stones and offerings, he said, 'As for these things which you see, the days will come when there shall not be left here one stone upon another that will not be thrown down'" (21:5–6).

MARTYR PROPHET

Prophets in the Bible give a variety of messages, but a typical message would be that people are not living the way they ought and will have trouble (again see Jer 7:1–20). The "will have trouble" part of this message is where biblical prophets connect with the description of their ability to speak of the future. If a person tells others they are not living the way they ought, what sort of emotional reaction might one expect? The anger prophets sometimes elicit in Israel has led to killing prophets. The long tradition of killing prophets finds expression in Elijah: "The Israelites have rejected your covenant, broken down your altars, and put your prophets to death with the sword. I am the only one left, and now they are trying to kill me too" (1 Kg 19:10).

Jesus in Luke's Gospel is presented as part of the martyr prophet tradition by confrontation: "'Woe to you, because you build tombs for the prophets, and it was your forefathers who killed them'" (Lk 11:47). Luke's Gospel also presents Jesus as identifying with the fate of a martyr prophet: "Herod wants to kill you."

He replied, "Go tell that fox, 'I will drive out demons and heal people today and tomorrow, and on the third day I will reach my goal.' In any case, I must keep going today and tomorrow and the next day—for surely no prophet can die outside Jerusalem!

"O Jerusalem, Jerusalem, you who kill the prophets and stone those sent to you, how often I have longed to gather your children together, as a hen gathers her chicks under her wings, but you were not willing!" (Lk 13: 31–34)

Jesus challenges and pays the price. His life is a witness to his faith in God, and his death establishes him in the company of prophets before him.

LIKE ELIJAH BUT GREATER

A further dimension of the theme of prophet is Jesus in the likeness of Elijah though greater. While in Mark and Matthew there are similarities between John and Baptist and Elijah, in Luke the similarity applies also to Jesus. As Elijah brings the widow's son back to life, so does Jesus (Lk 7:11+ parallels 1 Kgs 17:17+). Jewish belief generally includes expectation of Elijah's return. Elijah was not depicted as dying but as ascending into heaven (2 Kgs 2:11). Today at a Passover Seder, the Jewish meal celebrating God's interaction with the people of Israel, the door to the room is ajar, and there is an empty place setting or at least a goblet in expectation of the return of Elijah. Like Elijah, Luke's Gospel also has Jesus ascending to heaven (Lk 9:51; 24:51; Acts 1:9).

The likeness to Elijah has a limit as Luke appears to want to show Jesus as greater than Elijah. Elijah uses violence to enact God's will. The king in Samaria, Ahaziah fell and injured himself; he sent messengers to ask the God of Ekron his prognosis, but the God of Israel did not like this. He sent Elijah to meet the king's messengers to show them the power of the God of Israel. Elijah calls down fire from heaven upon the soldiers, killing 102 people (2 Kgs 2:1+). Luke chapter 9 Jesus is in Samaria and "sets his face toward Jerusalem," but the people of the village in Samaria would not show him hospitality. His disciples asked with expectation of Elijah-like behavior: "'Lord, do you want us to call fire down from heaven to destroy them?' But Jesus turned and rebuked them'" (Lk 9:54–55). This suggests that resorting to violence is not Jesus' way, and this makes him greater than Elijah.

One of the characteristics of biblical prophets is their tendency to challenge people. This ties in with what Crossan calls "parables of reversal" (53+). I will borrow from this early book of Crossan called *In Parables* to clarify one method of challenge contained in Jesus' parables.

Jesus challenged conventional values; the dynamic element in his presentation of the ruling power of God is the challenge to the hearer. These parables of reversal come from Luke's Gospel.

Jesus is asked by a lawyer (scribe) about eternal life; Jesus gives a parable of the good Samaritan (Lk 10) to explain who is the neighbor that the lawyer should love. The parable includes a man who was beaten up and left on the side of the road. A priest and then a Levite pass by the injured man without offering assistance. A Samaritan comes along and administers first aid and takes the injured person to an inn and gives the innkeeper money to take care of the man.

The lawyer would have identified with the priest and Levite as they all belong to the same religious establishment. Jesus makes the hero of the story the Samaritan, who would have been excluded from God's kingdom by the lawyer. Samaritans did not recognize the importance of Jerusalem and were regarded as half-breeds by many Jews. Samaria had been conquered by the Assyrians (2 Kings 17: 24–25, 29), so Samaritans were ethnically and religiously mixed, hence impure according to the Jewish establishment. Jews sometimes regarded Samaritans as idolaters (Josephus, *Antiquities*, 12.5.5). Josephus remembers times when Samaritans enslaved Jews (*Antiquities*, 12.6.1) and killed many Galileans (*Antiquities*, 20.6.1). Despite the enmity between Jews and Samaritans, Jesus makes a Samaritan the hero of this story. To make the Samaritan the hero of the story is to challenge the self-understanding of the lawyer who needs to change his understanding of God and Samaritans.

This parable takes what is conventionally considered bad (Samaritan), and makes it look good while taking what is conventionally good (priest) and making it look bad. This is the dynamic that is set in motion in the following parables of reversal (see Crossan 75+) .

LK 16:19+ PARABLE OF RICH MAN.

The rich man, conventionally regarded as good man ends in Hades; the poor man, conventionally regarded as bad, ends in the bosom of Abraham.

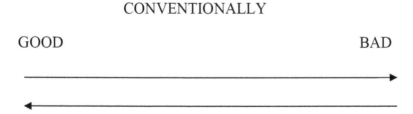

Figure 4.1. Conventionally Good vs. Bad

LK 18:10+ PHARISEE AND TAX COLLECTOR

Pharisee who was representative of good, prayed in self-exaltation, which was bad in the parable.

Tax collector, who was an image of a bad person as representative of foreign oppression, prayed in humble, hence good, way.

LK 14:12+ BANQUET GUESTS

Invite the poor and the lame ("bad") rather than the rich ("good").

LK 15:11+ PRODIGAL SON.

The older son was dutiful (good) but ended with resentment (bad); the younger son was wasteful (bad) but ended with good relationship with his father.

CHAMPION OF THE POOR

Jesus as prophet challenges inherited and customary thinking; his challenge was so severe that he was killed and entered the ranks of martyr prophets. Jesus' prophetic stance included not only his opposition to the conventional disdain for the poor but also his championing the poor. Only Luke opens Jesus' public ministry announcing his mission to the impoverished: "'The Spirit of the Lord is on me, because he has anointed me to preach good news to the poor'" (4:18). This good news has something to do with the biblical understanding of justice as he has numerous references to putting down the rich and raising up the poor.

In the Magnificat the Lord sends away the rich but fills the hungry: "He has brought down rulers from their thrones but has lifted up the humble. He has filled the hungry with good things but has sent the rich away empty" (Lk 1:52–53). Balancing of the scales expresses the principle of redress. In the classical and medieval worlds, justice was sometimes defined as giving each person his or her due (see, for example, Plato, *Republic*, I.332; Thomas Aquinas, *S.T.*, II-II, q. 58). In this way justice involves distribution, but by what criteria do God and society distribute? Two ways of distribution are according to what a person deserves and according to what a person needs. The Bible, according to Stephen Mott's *Biblical Ethics and Social Change*, favors the principle of need. God takes care of the needy, those who have lost their land and their health and wealth.

> The Lord . . . upholds the cause of the oppressed and gives food to the hungry. The Lord sets prisoners free, the Lord gives sight to the blind, the Lord lifts up those who are bowed down, the Lord loves the righteous. The Lord watches over the alien and sustains the fatherless and the widow, but he frustrates the ways of the wicked. (Ps 146:7–9; see Dt 10:18–19)

The Bible has numerous prophetic utterances against those who mistreat the poor: "The LORD enters into judgment against the elders and leaders of his people: It is you who have ruined my vineyard; the plunder from the poor is in your houses" (Is 3:14). Another is from Amos: "Hear this, you who trample the needy and do away with the poor of the land" (Amos 8:4).

The concern for the poor in Luke's Gospel continues the Hebraic prophetic traditions which attempt to protect the poor and warn those who have benefitted from plundering the poor. Luke's beatitude is "blessed are you poor" (Lk 6:20) instead of Matthew's more ambiguous "Blessed are the poor in spirit" (Mt 5:3). Not only does Luke give a number of sayings that support the poor, but he also deletes what could be used against the poor. (Contrast Mk 14:3+ with Luke 7:37+.)

It is not certain whether these are two versions of the same story or two stories that are similar. Nevertheless, the Markan line about "the poor you

Table 4.3. Mark 14:3–7 and Luke 7:37–39

Mark 14:3–7	Luke 7:37–39
[3]While he was in Bethany, reclining at the table in the home of a man known as Simon the Leper, a woman came with an alabaster jar of very expensive perfume, made of pure nard. She broke the jar and poured the perfume on his head. [4]Some of those present were saying indignantly to one another, "Why this waste of perfume? [5]It could have been sold for more than a year's wages and the money given to the poor." And they rebuked her harshly. [6]"Leave her alone," said Jesus. "Why are you bothering her? She has done a beautiful thing to me. [7]The poor you will always have with you, and you can help them any time you want. But you will not always have me."	[37]When a woman who had lived a sinful life in that town learned that Jesus was eating at the Pharisee's house, she brought an alabaster jar of perfume, [38]and as she stood behind him at his feet weeping, she began to wet his feet with her tears. Then she wiped them with her hair, kissed them and poured perfume on them. [39]When the Pharisee who had invited him saw this, he said to himself, "If this man were a prophet, he would know who is touching him and what kind of woman she is—that she is a sinner."

always have with you" was not something Luke chose to use, as it could diminish concern for the poor.

MODEL OF PRAYER

Jesus as a prophet becomes a model of prayer in Luke. At significant events in his story, Luke shows Jesus praying. He prays before his baptism (3:21), before choosing twelve apostles (6:12), before the confession of Peter (9:18), before the transfiguration (9:28), before the giving of the Lord's Prayer (11:1), and before his arrest (22:41). Except for the prayer in the Garden of Gethsemane, all of these scenes of Jesus praying are unique to Luke's version. With Jesus as model of prayer, he repeatedly asks disciples to pray also (11:1+; 18:1+). Jesus who has an unparalleled position among people in the minds of Christians spent all night in prayer (6:12) according to Luke. His example contains a challenge to his followers.

INNOCENT AND MERCIFUL SAVIOR

The word "savior" occurs only three times in the four Gospels, including twice in Luke's Gospel plus twice in his Acts of the Apostles; Jesus is called savior early in Luke's Gospel: "Today in the town of David a Savior has been born to you; he is Christ the Lord" (2:11; also Acts 5:31; 13:23).

It is noteworthy that Caesar Augustus is mentioned in Luke's infancy narrative (2:1). Caesar Augustus was widely known as "savior of the world," as found in a Greek inscription from Preine (in current Turkey):

> Since providence, which has ordered all things of our life and is very much interested in our life, has ordered things in sending Augustus, whom she filled with virtue for the benefit of men, sending him as a *savior* both for us and for those after us, him who would end war and order all things, and since Caesar by his appearance surpassed the hopes of all those who received the good tidings, not only those who were benefactors before him, but even the hope among those who will be left afterward, and the birthday of the god was for the world the beginning of the good tidings through him; and Asia resolved it in Smyrna. (http://www.textexcavation.com/augustus.html)

Luke is subversively suggesting that Jesus is not the same kind of savior as Caesar Augustus. Jesus is not trying to overthrow the government. Luke has Roman living compatible with Christian living, but he looked beyond civil order.

An understanding of Jesus' saving activity is partially disclosed in the word "to save" which often is identical in Luke to the word "heal" (e.g., 8:48; 18:42).

One may stretch the concept to include the healing impact Jesus had on people through his compassion. On the cross one of the criminals dying next to Jesus asks for Jesus' help: "Then he said, 'Jesus, remember me when you come into your kingdom.' Jesus answered him, 'I tell you the truth, today you will be with me in paradise'" (Lk 23:42–43). Here Jesus' saving action implies life after death as well as merciful expression in the time of need of the criminal, despite Jesus' own suffering.

Mercy is a theme that runs throughout Luke's Gospel. Instead of Matthew's chapter 5 "Be perfect," Luke gives "be merciful": a less ambiguous demand. Only Luke has the prodigal son parable where the father expresses mercy toward his returning son. The lost sheep and coin parables are only in Luke (ch. 15) and show mercy by not condemning sinners. The focus of the sinful woman who washes Jesus' feet with her tears is mercy (Lk 7:36+).

Mercy and salvation are plainly intertwined; Luke has Jesus extend "salvation" to Zacchaeus, who had two strikes against him, a tax collector and wealthy (Lk 19). Though the word "mercy" does not occur there, Jesus does not condemn the man who was cooperating with Rome and would have been regarded as less than honest by his contemporaries.

Jesus, in the course of being arrested shows mercy to the arresting officer by healing his ear (Lk 22:51) and offers merciful forgiveness to those engaged in killing him: "'Father, forgive them, for they do not know what they are doing'" (Lk 23:34).

INNOCENT

The dignity and innocence of Jesus give special meaning to his death in Luke's Gospel. Surely Jesus was regarded to be of exalted character by his followers; he resists temptation, serves the outcasts, counsels mercy, but in Luke minor details help to elevate him and protect his image. The arrest of Jesus will help to bring out some of these details.

Notice the difference in the rank of the people arresting Jesus. In Mark's version shows a crowd sent from the high-ranking people (43), whereas in Luke the high-ranking officials came themselves (52). The difference in rank expresses deference toward the importance of Jesus.

In Mark Jesus is kissed by Judas; in Luke the kiss is not depicted, only Judas' intention. Before Judas can act Jesus confronts him with precognitive power: "'Judas, are you betraying the Son of Man with a kiss?'" (48). The

Table 4.4. Mark 14:43–50 and Luke 22:47–54

Mark 14:43–50	*Luke 22:47–54*
[43]"Just as he was speaking, Judas, one of the Twelve, appeared. With him was a crowd armed with swords and clubs, sent from the chief priests, the teachers of the law, and the elders. [44]Now the betrayer had arranged a signal with them: 'The one I kiss is the man; arrest him and lead him away under guard.' [45]Going at once to Jesus, Judas said, 'Rabbi!' and kissed him. [46]The men seized Jesus and arrested him. [47]Then one of those standing near drew his sword and struck the servant of the high priest, cutting off his ear. [48]'Am I leading a rebellion,' said Jesus, 'that you have come out with swords and clubs to capture me? [49]Every day I was with you, teaching in the temple courts, and you did not arrest me. But the Scriptures must be fulfilled.' [50]Then everyone deserted him and fled. [50]They seized him . . . "	[47]"While he was still speaking a crowd came up, and the man who was called Judas, one of the Twelve, was leading them. He approached Jesus to kiss him, [48]but Jesus asked him, 'Judas, are you betraying the Son of Man with a kiss?' [49]When Jesus' followers saw what was going to happen, they said, 'Lord, should we strike with our swords?' [50]And one of them struck the servant of the high priest, cutting off his right ear. [51]But Jesus answered, 'No more of this!' And he touched the man's ear and healed him. [52]Then Jesus said to the chief priests, the officers of the temple guard, and the elders, who had come for him, 'Am I leading a rebellion that you have come with swords and clubs? [53]Every day I was with you in the temple courts, and you did not lay a hand on me. But this is your hour—when darkness reigns.' [54]Then they seized him and led him away . . . "

status of Jesus is further acknowledged when the disciples ask permission and address him as Lord, a sign of respect (49).

The merciful Jesus puts an end to violence and heals the wounded soldier (51). Finally, he hands himself over showing greater control of the scene than in Mark. At the same time he acknowledges the power of evil at work through the scene (Satan had entered into Judas at the beginning of ch. 22, leading to betrayal and here arrest), and so shows a breadth of perspective transcending the other characters in the scene.

The cumulative effect of these small details helps to elevate the dignity of Jesus. This adds to the impact of his death.

Recall the impact of the death of Jesus in Mark and Matthew. In Mark the death triggers the moment of recognition. In Matthew the tombs open, thus fulfilling Jewish hope from Ezekiel 37. Though Matthew has a moment of recognition, it is less central as is fulfilling prophecy with tombs opening and rocks splitting. In Luke something else occurs which fits the portrayal Luke has been painting.

In Luke's presentation of the crucifixion, Jesus is declared innocent. In the preceding chapter, Jesus is declared innocent by Pilate a number of times, probably to show the Roman official in a comparatively positive light to

Table 4.5. Mark 15:38–39, Matthew 27:51–54, and Luke 23:45–49 (RSV)

Mark 15:38–39	Matthew 27:51–54	Luke 23:45–49 (RSV)
³⁸The curtain of the temple was torn in two from top to bottom. ³⁹And when the centurion, who stood there in front of Jesus, heard his cry and saw how he died, he said, "Surely this man was the Son of God!"	⁵¹At that moment the curtain of the temple was torn in two from top to bottom. The earth shook and the rocks split. ⁵²The tombs broke open and the bodies of many holy people who had died were raised to life. ⁵³They came out of the tombs, and after Jesus' resurrection they went into the holy city and appeared to many people. ⁵⁴When the centurion and those with him who were guarding Jesus saw the earthquake and all that had happened, they were terrified, and exclaimed, "Surely he was the Son of God."	⁴⁵While the sun's light failed; and the curtain of the temple was torn in two. ⁴⁶Then Jesus, crying with a loud voice, said, "Father, into thy hands I commit my spirit!" And having said this he breathed his last. ⁴⁷Now when the centurion saw what had taken place, he praised God, and said, "Certainly this man was innocent!" ⁴⁸And all the multitudes who assembled to see the sight, when they saw what had taken place, returned home beating their breasts. ⁴⁹And all his acquaintances and the women who had followed him from Galilee stood at a distance and saw these things.

demonstrate compatibility between Christian life and life under Roman rule. The innocence of Jesus in the crucifixion, however, has an impact on the audience. Those who witnessed the scene left "beating their breasts" (48). Beating of breasts in Isaiah 32:12 expresses mourning. The impact of the death of Jesus in Luke's Gospel is remorse. The death of an innocent man, sometimes depicted in world literature (consider Melville's *Billy Budd* or Dostoyevsky's *The Idiot*), shows the horror of sin and the depravity of humanity. The impact of the death of Jesus in Luke is sorrow. This sadness also occurs in the denial of Peter shortly before Jesus' death:

> Peter replied, "Man, I don't know what you're talking about!" Just as he was speaking, the rooster crowed. The Lord turned and looked straight at Peter. Then Peter remembered the word the Lord had spoken to him: "Before the rooster crows today, you will disown me three times." And he went outside and wept bitterly. (Luke 22:60–62)

The sorrow of Peter is generated by the look of Jesus, just as the sorrow of the crucifixion witnesses is triggered by Jesus' death.

Jesus in Luke is a martyr prophet, whose compassion, innocence, and dignity intensify the tragedy of his death. Here again Jesus is a subversive figure whose image is not designed to overthrow Roman rule and thereby subject his followers to attack but rather to put things in their proper order where neither Caesar, nor Jewish leaders, nor conventional values have ultimacy.

Chapter 5

Jesus in John's Gospel

Political Activist, Pre-existent Word of God, the I Am of Hebrew Tradition, Replacement of Jewish Patriarchs, and the Father's Offer of Life

Key questions to help with discovery of Jesus in John's Gospel:

1. Where else in the Bible does one read the opening words of John's Gospel?
2. What in the world of the Bible would be a likely meaning of "Through him all things were made; without him nothing was made that has been made" (Jn 1)?
3. Why might John have not included the temptation of Jesus, the baptism of Jesus, and the agony in the Garden of Gethsemane?
4. What do the terms "bread of life," "true vine," and "good shepherd" have in common?
5. How is the portrayal of Jesus in the baptism scene in John's Gospel different from that in the Gospels of Matthew, Mark, and Luke?

Discussion questions:

1. What in the dialog with the Samaritan woman (Jn 4) would have contemporary relevance?
2. How might one avoid anti-Semitic interpretation of John's Gospel?

JESUS AS POLITICAL ACTIVIST IN JOHN'S GOSPEL

Jesus in John's Gospel is entangled in a resistance movement so evident in the Synoptics. This resistance movement contrasts with the Judean rulers who run the Temple and cooperate with Rome. Jesus performs mighty deeds outside of Jerusalem: in Galilee (2:11; 4:49–54) and Samaria (4:7–4:42) as well in Jerusalem (7:28–31). His works were generating allegiance to him (2:11; 4:42; 7:31).

The growing popularity of Jesus generated fear among those in charge of the Temple state:

> Many of the Judeans therefore, who had come with Mary and had seen what he did, believed in him; but some of them went to the Pharisees and told them what Jesus had done. So the chief priests and the Pharisees gathered the council, and said, "What are we to do? For this man performs many signs. If we let him go on thus, everyone will believe in him, and the Romans will come and destroy both our holy place and our nation." (Jn 11:45–48)

Jesus talks about replacing the Temple with the Samaritan woman (ch. 4), that plus his growing popularity, his obstructing Temple commerce (ch. 2:14–21), and the crowds calling him King of Israel (12:13) led to his arrest and death.

John's Gospel is different from the Gospels of Matthew, Mark, and Luke in style and content. John is filled with lofty theology. As a result of theological richness John's Gospel has been studied as a treasure chest for theological assertions, but Jesus in his political reality is easily overlooked. For that reason, it would be worthwhile to trace the political story of Jesus throughout John's Gospel. Jesus as a prophet in conflict with the Temple state is remarkably coherent with the agent of God described in the first chapter of this reading guide on the One Jesus and Many and also found in the Matthew, Mark, and Luke.

Chapter after chapter his activism is generating both a growing following of believers as well as a growing sense of threat by those who are running the Temple state. In chapter 1, Jesus gathers his disciples along with a plateful of titles: Rabbi, Son of God, King of Israel (1:49). In chapter 2, Jesus provides an abundance of wine which is associated with God's restoration: "For behold, in those days and at that time, when I restore the fortunes of Judah and Jerusalem. . . . And in that day the mountains shall drip sweet wine . . . " (Joel 3:1, 18). This event is contrasted with Jesus' trip to the Temple in Jerusalem where he interfered with money changing: "he poured out the coins of the money-changers and overturned their tables . . . " He prophetically announced, "You shall not make my Father's house a house of trade." He went on to declare of the destruction of the Temple (John 2:13–22). Passover as a time of celebration of Hebrew liberation was now a time when poor people needed to pay to offer sacrifice, and with Jesus it became a time of confrontation which caused many to believe in him (2:23). In chapters 3 and 4, Jesus takes over the activity of baptizing, showing both his connection to John the Baptist as well as his superiority. In chapter 4, he passes through Samaria and speaks of replacement of the Temple with worship in Spirit and Truth. This would have been a threat to those who are profiting from the Temple. In Samaria he impresses both the woman at the well as well as the townspeople who believed in him (4:39–42). His popularity is presented as growing along with his challenges to the Temple state and its supporters. In chapter 5, Jesus goes to Jerusalem and heals a man. In reaction to this, some Judeans wanted to kill him because he broke Sabbath law and called God his Father (John 5:1–18). In chapter 6, Jesus returns to Galilee and takes the idea that Moses had fed the Hebrews in the desert and ascribes the feeding to his Father. He not only challenged the Temple but here challenged the story told at Passover (6:32–33). In chapter 7, he returns to Jerusalem despite the danger of being killed (7:1). He was a cause of division as some thought he was a good man, but others thought he was "leading the people astray" (7:10–12). After arguments about his authority, the chief priests and Pharisees sought to arrest him (7:32), but they do not as some Temple officers were positively impressed with his words (7:46). Chapter 8 continues with intense disputes about Jesus' identity. In chapter 9, Jesus' healing of a blind man brings out divided responses: some see and believe, others do not. Chapter 10 describes similar division as Jesus' claims to be a good shepherd (10: 7,19–21). Jesus claiming to be life giver (5:16–18; 10:28) provokes lethal hostility (5:18; 10:31). Raising Lazarus from the dead led the Pharisees and chief priests to seek to have him arrested (11:47–48, 57). In chapter 12, a crowd proclaims Jesus king of Israel (12:12), a title he never used. In ch. 13–17, Jesus gives a new commandment to his disciples as he says farewell. He is arrested and is condemned for posing as king of the Jews and as son of God as a threat to the rule of the Roman son of God, Caesar. Even after the resurrection the disciples are hiding out of fear of the authorities (20:19). Jesus appears in order to continue what he had begun (20:21).

How much of this is rooted in history is widely debated, but the story of Jesus as one who challenged the practices and authority of the Temple state runs through John's Gospel as it does the other Gospels. If anything, Jesus appears to be more of a threat because he attracted followers throughout Galilee and Judah (for more of this type of reading of John, see Horsley, *John, Jesus, and the Renewal of Israel*, ch. 5).

OTHER CONFLICTS

The conflict with the rulers of Israel over religious practice (e.g., Sabbath) so prominent in the Synoptics is not the only source of discord and danger. John's Gospel also gives attention to higher Christological disputes.

John's Jesus is the pre-existent Word of God (John 1:1–14) who expects to return to his Father (6:62). His claim to be one with God generates conflict between Jesus and the leaders of the Jewish community (5:17–18; 8:57–9; 10:33).

John's Gospel offers support to Jewish Christians who have lost their connection to their synagogues and have to find unity with Gentiles who also follow Jesus. "The Jews had already agreed that if anyone should confess him to be Christ, he was to be put out of the synagogue" (Jn 9:22; also 12:42). John is focusing on Jesus in part to support and reassure those Jewish Christians. John aims to clarify who Jesus is by bringing together both Mediterranean wisdom speculation and Jewish monotheism: Jesus is the Word (*logos*) of God. John furthers this project by using the most exalted religious language available in his culture to apply to Jesus: Jesus is the "I Am" from Exodus.

"THE JEWS" IN JOHN'S GOSPEL

In John's Gospel "the Jews" are sometimes depicted as opponents to Jesus. "And this was why the Jews persecuted Jesus, because he did this on the Sabbath" (5:16). John uses the word *Ioudaioi*: "All the references to *Ioudaioi* in John denote Judeans, largely a territorial term, with exception of the instances in Samaria (in John 4), where 'Jews' has 'the correct denotation, but lacks the connotation of Judea,'" Culpepper, R. A. "The Gospel of John and the Jews," *Review and Expositor* 84, no. 2 (1987): 273–288.

The word "Jews" in John's Gospel would often better be translated as "Judeans," an ethnic group with some associations to geography, a group that maintained traditional customs and modes of worship; ethnicity was inseparable from religion. In the third century this word became the name of a religious group when religion could be separated from its ethnic context (see Mason, S., *Josephus, Judea, and Christian Origins*, Ada, MI: Baker Academic, 2008, 152).

The word "Jews" in John's Gospel does not refer to all "Jews" but mainly to those people living in Israel who were opposed to Jesus' teaching (Moloney, Francis, J., *The Gospel of John*, Collegeville, MN: Liturgical Press, 1998, 10–11).

WORD OF GOD

The first chapter of John's Gospel presents Jesus as the Word of God through whom all things came to be. "In the beginning" evokes the first book of the Bible in which God created the heavens and the earth. In the first chapter of Genesis, God creates by speaking. Thus, according to the Hebrew Scriptures all things came into being through God's creative word. This word takes flesh in Jesus according to John 1:14. This is a big step beyond Matthew, Mark, and Luke. This is not to say Jesus is not put forth as Divine in those Gospels, but in John's Gospel Jesus is associated with the creation of all things.

Imagine meeting Jesus, a charismatic preacher, a healer, a man with profound wisdom. If a person witnessed a spectacular healing, that person would be unlikely to immediately conclude that all creation came from that healer. How might John have come to the insight linking Jesus to all of creation?

The Jesus encountered by people uttered words of wisdom. His ability to out debate his rivals, and his pithy sayings led some to see him as the very spokesperson for Divine wisdom. Luke has Jesus associated with wisdom: "Because of this, God in his wisdom said, 'I will send them prophets and apostles, some of whom they will kill and others they will persecute'" (Lk 11:49). In Matthew, Jesus is identified with Wisdom: "Therefore I am sending you prophets and wise men and teachers. Some of them you will kill and crucify" (Mt 23:34).

The wise words of Jesus were embodied in his life. He spoke about embracing outcasts, for example, and he lived that message. Jesus was admired in part because there was not a wide gap between his words and his deeds. Jesus' life embodied Divine wisdom.

How would John link Jesus as the embodiment of God's wisdom with the creation of all things? Proverbs 8 appears to be the simplest explanation. In Proverbs 8 the wisdom of God speaks: "Does not wisdom call out?" (Proverbs 8:1). Word and wisdom are thus somewhat interchangeable here and in the prologue to John's Gospel. Proverbs 8 gives another element, namely the Wisdom of God is personified as a master craftsman present in God's creative work. "Then I was the craftsman at his side. I was filled with delight day after day, rejoicing always in his presence, rejoicing in his whole world and delighting in mankind" (Proverbs 8:30–31). John identifies this Wisdom of God with Jesus, a man who so profoundly embodied the wisdom associated with God that he became identified with it. This is not to say that Jesus exhausted God's Wisdom, but he manifested it clearly.

Speculations about Divine Wisdom and word (*logos*) were present among Greeks: "The passive principle, then, is a substance without quality, i.e., matter, whereas the active is the reason [*logos*] inherent in this substance, that is God. For he is everlasting and is the artificer of each several thing throughout the whole extent of matter" (Diogenes Laertius, *Lives of Eminent Philosophers*, VII, 134) and Jews: "The incorporeal world then was already completed, having its seat in the Divine Reason [=*logos*]; and the world, perceptible by the external senses, was made on the model of it; and the first portion of it, being also the most excellent of all made by the Creator, was the heaven . . . " (Philo, *On the Creation*, X.36) John's contribution is to identify the *logos* with Jesus.

John, in the prologue of his Gospel, presents Jesus as the resting place of Wisdom that has come down from above. Wisdom in Jewish literature had sought a resting place but was rejected. "Wisdom found not a place on earth where she could inhabit; her dwelling therefore is in heaven. Wisdom went forth to dwell among the sons of men, but she obtained not a habitation. Wisdom returned to her place, and seated herself in the midst of the angels" (Enoch 42). Jesus experienced rejection as did some of his Jewish readers who were being evicted from synagogues (Jn 9:22, 12:42, 16:2): "He was in the world, and the world was made through him, yet the world did not know him. He came to his own, and his own people did not receive him" (John 1:10–11, ESV). Despite rejection, Wisdom finds a home in the world: "But to all who did receive him, who believed in his name, he gave the right to become children of God. . . . And the Word became flesh and dwelt among us . . . " (Jn 1:12, 14).

If linking Wisdom from Proverbs 8 with Jesus in John 1 does not completely establish the note of "pre-existence," John makes this evident later in his Gospel where he has Jesus say: "You are from below; I am from above. You are of this world; I am not of this world" (8:23). Jesus is the pre-existent Word/Wisdom of God. This assertion makes Jesus stand out from the rest of humanity.

I AM

Jesus in John's Gospel utters the words "I Am" in ways that call attention to himself. In chapter 8, in his argument with his opponents, he says, "Before Abraham was I Am." Obviously we would say, "Before Abraham was I was," but John has this strange wording. The same words come out in the arrest scene in chapter 18. Judas and some soldiers and officials came to arrest Jesus. Jesus asks who they want, and he identifies himself as Jesus of Nazareth by saying "I Am." When the soldiers and officials heard him say "I Am" they "fell to the ground." This is not the usual response of arresting officers! Though some translations have Jesus saying, "I am he," the words in Greek are simply *ego eimi* [εγω ειμι], the same found in chapter 8: "Before

Abraham was I Am." What is this strange language that violates ordinary grammar and evokes such a reaction in arresting officers?

This unusual language comes from the book of Exodus. There Moses is walking in the desert, and he sees a bush that is burning and hears a voice from the bush. The God of the Israelites speaks to Moses, directing him to go to Pharaoh to free the people of Israel from Egyptian slavery. In anticipation of the questioning of the Israelites, Moses asks the name of the God. The NIV of Exodus 3:14–15 gives the Divine self-disclosure:

> God said to Moses, "I Am who I Am. This is what you are to say to the Israelites: 'I AM has sent me to you.'"
>
> God also said to Moses, "Say to the Israelites, 'The LORD, the God of your fathers—the God of Abraham, the God of Isaac and the God of Jacob—has sent me to you.' This is my name forever, the name by which I am to be remembered from generation to generation."

Thanks to Samuel Terrien, who includes some of the Hebrew here, we can appreciate some added meaning. His version is as follows:

> And Moses said to the Elohim, "Behold when I come to the sons of Israel and I say to them, The Elohim of your fathers has sent me toward you, and if they say, 'What is his name?' What shall I say unto them?" (3:13)
>
> And Elohim said to Moses, "*Eheyeh 'asher eheyeh.*" And he said, "Thus wilt thou say to the sons of Israel, *'Eheyeh* has sent me to you."
>
> And Elohim said again to Moses, "Thus wilt thou say to the sons of Israel, Yahweh, The Elohim of your fathers, the Elohim of Abraham, the Elohim of Isaac, and the Elohim of Jacob has sent me to you. This is my name forever. And this is my memorial for generation of generation." (Exodus 3:14–15; Terrien, *The Elusive Presence*, 114)

The names of God in this text are twofold. The first is "I am who am" or "I Am" for short. The text then uses the word "*Yahweh*" meaning, "he who is" which appears to be a synonym for the "I Am" name.

"I Am" is not a name that gives the hearer very much information. It does not disclose much as Terrien's title suggests, it speaks of an "elusive presence." If on the first day of first grade all the children have name tags, and a child has a name tag with a capital letter "I," that child is going to have trouble. "I" is a name we give to ourselves, not a name to offer to another person. We do not call others "I." How could God be addressed in the first person? This conundrum suggests mysterious presence and Divine indefinability. "Why do you ask my name? It is beyond understanding" (Judges 13:18). The Israelites used these words with great reverence and reticence.

To this day many Jews do not use these names out of a fear of misusing the names, hence blaspheming.

At some point after the Babylonian exile, *Adonai,* meaning "Lord" was used as a circumlocution for YHWH (Parke-Taylor 9+). The Lord is the role or occupation of God rather than His name. He is Lord of heaven and earth. Throughout the Bible the word Lord substitutes for the name Yahweh. The name of God was written without vowels. Those who created the Masoretic Text (6th–10th century C.E.) replaced the vowels of the name YHWH with the vowels of Adonai: a,o,a most likely to avoid misuse of God's name. If one inserts a, o, a into the consonants YHWH the result is YaHoWa which is close to our English Yahowa or Jehovah, a name which is not a truly Hebrew word but a conflation of two Hebrew words.

Early Christian usage helped to determine Christian pronunciation. Clement of Alexandria, (2nd–3rd century) for example, writes, "The mystic name of four letters . . . is called Jave, which is interpreted 'Who is and shall be'" (Clement of Alexandria, *Stromata*, 5.6). In Greek this would be Ἰαουε, which is phonetically equivalent to the English Yahweh.

Pronunciation is not the real problem here. If we are interested in John's Gospel, what is the meaning of "I Am" as a name for God in relation to YHWH? Most simply one name is in the first person and the other is in the third. According to Parke-Taylor's *Yahweh: The Divine Name in the Bible.* "I am who am" (*Eheyeh 'asher eheyeh.*) of Exodus 3:14 as an explanation for the Divine name YHWH found in verse 15 "I am" refers to identity and expresses existence (50+). Exodus 3:14 "brings into focus the importance of the verb 'to be'" (51). This position emphasizes the link between *hyh* of YHWH as derived from the verb "to be" over any attempt to introduce the idea of creation or causation.

The "I Am" of Exodus 3:14 (*ego eimi* in the Septuagint) in Greek is identical to the I Am of John 8:58 and 18:5–6. The I Am stressed the uniqueness of God in other parts of the Hebrew scriptures: "I am the Lord, and there is no other" (Is 45:18). It also functioned as a name: "I, I Am he that comforts you" (Is 51:12). In the Septuagint this is "I am I Am" *(ego eimi ego eimi,* ἐγώ εἰμι, ἐγώ εἰμι; this is from the Tischendorf text available online). Capital letters clarify: I am I Am. (Brown's *The Gospel According to John I–XII* has an excellent appendix on I Am 533+.)

The mysterious presence of God revealed to Moses along with the name so sacred that people rarely pronounced it, is given to Jesus in John's Gospel. To say Jesus is Yahweh is not going beyond John. Jesus is Lord, in the highest sense. It is no wonder that this attribution shocked many Jews.

REPLACEMENT OF JEWISH PATRIARCHS

John's Gospel contains the dynamic of replacement. Throughout the Gospel, something new replaces something old or something superior replaces something inferior. At the wedding feast of Cana in chapter 2, for example, wine replaces water. With the Samaritan woman in chapter 4, mountain worship is replaced by worship in spirit and truth (Ellis 1984 gives extended treatment of replacement in *The Genius of John*).

This replacement activity applies to the Jewish patriarchs in a variety of places. As early as John 1:17, John the Baptist is portrayed as proclaiming the law came through Moses, but grace and truth come through Jesus. At the well associated with the patriarch Jacob, Jesus and the women dialog about living water. The surface meaning of living water is flowing water or healthy water; Jesus speaks of a greater water than that coming from the well. The woman questions: "Are you greater than our father Jacob, who gave us the well?" (John 4:12). Jesus here shifts the meaning of living water to eternal life: "the water I give him will become in him a spring of water welling up to eternal life." In chapter 8, Jesus engages in bitter polemic with some Jewish opponents, and they ask if he is greater than Abraham. Here Jesus replies with the language of "before Abraham was I Am."

The theme of replacement in John's Gospel has carried an unfortunate consequence of anti-Jewish thinking. When Jesus is arguing with some Jews, many Christians throughout history have mistakenly seen the Jews there as representing all Jews. Since Jesus and his first disciples were Jews, simple logic would lead a rational reader to see these "Jews" as those who did not agree with Jesus or John's understanding of Jesus. (See Moloney 9+ for more on this.) As mentioned in the chapter on Matthew's Gospel, early Christianity often used "replacement" to show its superiority to the more dominant religion at that time in order to gain market share. That move in its time made sense, but obviously Christianity is no longer a fledgling religion needing to establish itself by odious contrast.

FATHER'S OFFER OF LIFE

In John's Gospel, Jesus refers to himself more than 100 times while in the Synoptic Gospels there are far fewer. A recurring instance of Jesus referring to himself relates to life. A concise statement of these self-references of Jesus comes from John 5:21: "For just as the Father raises the dead and gives them life, even so the Son gives life to whom he is pleased to give it." The Son as life giver in John itemizes ways he supports and protects life.

6:35, 48: "I am the bread of life"—nourishment, nourishing life
6:51: "I am the living bread"
8:12: "I am the light of the world"—guidance
10:7: "I am the door of the sheep (sheep gate)"—protection
10:11: "I am the good shepherd"
11:25: "I am the resurrection and the life"—eternal life
14:6: "I am the way, the truth, and the life"
15:1: "I am the true vine"—source of life

These self-designations show Jesus as the source of protection, guidance, and life itself.

JESUS AS MINISTER OF SACRAMENTS

There is a strong ecclesial strain in John's Gospel that includes sacraments of Baptism and Eucharist. The language of "eating flesh" and "drinking blood" of chapter 6 are sacramental. (For those who dispute the sacramental references in John, see Brown 1997, 377+.) How could "drinking blood" be a metaphor for accepting Jesus' teaching when that action would have been a horror to those formed in the biblical tradition (see Brown, 1966, 284+)? The baptismal element in John deserves more attention as it is part of a historical development easily seen in the other gospels.

If one looks at the treatment of Jesus being baptized in the Gospel, one notices changes from early to later gospels. A chart will make these changes easier to see.

After these parallel passages in the Synoptics, John adds material that radically changes the picture.

Before dealing with those changes, notice what happens from Mark to Matthew. Assuming the priority of Mark, we see in Mark a simple description of Jesus being baptized by John within a baptism of repentance. This scene posed two problems for early Christianity. Firstly it puts Jesus in a subordinate role to John the Baptist. Secondly, why would the sinless Jesus be entering into a baptism of repentance?

Matthew handles the first problem by having Jesus and John the Baptist engage in a conversation about the inappropriateness of the situation and agree to do what is fitting. "I need to be baptized by you, and do you come to me?" This does not deal with the situation of a sinless Jesus present at the baptism, but it at least acknowledges the discomfort of the early Christian community with Jesus in a subordinate role. After all, the Gospel of Luke acknowledges some rivalry between Jesus and John the Baptist among the disciples. "Lord, teach us to pray, just as John taught his disciples" (Lk 11:1).

Table 5.1. Mark 1:9–11, Matthew 3:13–17, Luke 3:21–22, and John 3:22–23; 4:1–2

Mark 1:9–11	*Matthew 3:13–17*	*Luke 3:21–22*	*John 3:22–23; 4:1–2*
In those days Jesus came from Nazareth of Galilee and was baptized by John in the Jordan. And when he came up out of the water, immediately he saw the heavens opened and the Spirit descending upon him like a dove, and a voice came from heaven, "Thou art my beloved Son; with thee I am well pleased."	Then Jesus came from Galilee to the Jordan to John, to be baptized by him. John would have prevented him, saying, "I need to be baptized by you, and do you come to me?" But Jesus answered him, "Let it be so now, for thus it is fitting for us to fulfill all righteousness." Then he consented. And when Jesus was baptized, he went up immediately from the water, and behold, the heavens were opened, and he saw the spirit of God descending like a dove, and alighting on him; and low a voice from heaven, saying, "This is my beloved Son, with whom I am well pleased."	Now when all the people were baptized, and when Jesus also had been baptized and was praying, the heaven was opened, and the Holy Spirit descended upon him in bodily form, as a dove, and a voice came from heaven, "Thou art my beloved Son; with thee I am well pleased."	After this Jesus and his disciples went into the land of Judea; there he remained with them and baptized. John also was baptizing at Aenon near Salim, because there was much water there; and people came and were baptized. Now when the Lord knew that the Pharisees had heard that Jesus was making and baptizing more disciples than John (although Jesus himself did not baptize, but only his disciples), and he left Judea and departed again to Galilee.

Matthew makes undeniable that Jesus is subordinating himself to John the Baptist for some grander purpose. Luke's treatment tones down John's role slightly by saying "when Jesus also had been baptized" rather than Mark's "by John."

John's Gospel does not have Jesus baptized at all in chapter 1. In chapter 3:22–23, Jesus is baptizing, and John the Baptist is an afterthought: "After this, Jesus and his disciples went out into the Judean countryside, where he spent some time with them, and baptized. Now John also was baptizing." Here there is no question of Jesus subordinating himself to John the Baptist in a ritual designed for penitents. John's Gospel goes further in chapter 4 by denying that Jesus baptizes, which he just affirmed in the previous chapter.

"The Pharisees heard that Jesus was gaining and baptizing more disciples than John, although in fact it was not Jesus who baptized, but his disciples" (John 4:1–2).

Not only is Jesus not baptized by John the Baptist, but he is outperforming John the Baptist and is a kind of executive over the baptizing enterprise. Jesus is not even getting his hands wet. In John, Jesus is removed from whatever controversy one might see in Mark, Matthew, and Luke.

As the picture of Jesus in relation to baptism shows, John's Jesus is a person of authority. John's Gospel does not contain Jesus' baptism, and also does not present his temptation in the desert, his agony in the Garden of Gethsemane, or his crying out from the cross: "My God, why have you forsaken me?" His titles "I Am" and "Word of God" give foundation to that authority. His function as life giver shows him as an answer to human desire. His political activism shows this authority did not come easily.

Chapter 6

Paul

Christ Crucified, Last Adam, Life-Giving Spirit, Freedom and the Law, Source of Unity, Redeemer, and Lord

Key questions to help with discovery of Paul's understanding of Jesus:

1. Why does Paul contrast worldly wisdom with the wisdom he preaches in 1 Corinthians 1?
2. What is his reason for cautioning Corinthian Christians against engaging in lawsuits with each other?
3. If there are no other gods, why is Paul against eating meat that has been sacrificed to gods at a pagan temple?
4. How might the poor be humiliated at the Eucharist in 1 Corinthians 11:22?
5. Why does Paul prefer prophecy to speaking in tongues in chapter 14?
6. If obedience to Jewish Law is a questionable path, to what source of guidance does Paul point in Romans 8?
7. How according to the Letter to the Romans, can Jewish and Gentile Christians find unity?

Discussion questions:

1. What contemporary implications might one find in Paul's utterance: "the written code kills" (2 Cor 3)?
2. In 1 Corinthians 7:29 Paul discusses marriage and says " the time has grown short"; what does that say about his understanding of reality?

In the midst changing fortunes for Jewish and Gentile Christians, Paul offers both groups hope beyond their differences in their common need for God in Jesus.

JESUS AND PAUL

Paul did not meet Jesus of Nazareth in the flesh. He rather had a mystical encounter with the Risen Christ which altered the direction of his life which he then dedicated to preaching to Gentiles.

Paul does acknowledge having encountered people who were Christian before he was: "Greet Andronicus and Junia, my relatives and my fellow prisoners; they are prominent among the apostles and they were in Christ before me" (Rm 16:7). Though there is no evidence suggesting he heard Jesus preaching, he may have learned from these early Christians, e.g., non-retaliation: "When reviled we bless" (1 Cor 4:12); "Overcome evil with good" (Rm 12:21).

Paul and Jesus had different relationships with the Temple: Jesus is presented as confronting the way the Temple was functioning and as predicting its destruction (Mk 13). These tensions link Jesus to a national interest, namely Israel is in a national emergency overrun by Gentile rule. Paul shows no such national interest in his mission to the Gentiles.

Paul gives several references to Jesus in his writing (taken from Akenson, D. H., *Saint Saul*, Oxford: Oxford University Press, 2000, 226+):

1. Jesus was born by normal process (Rm 1:3); 2. The "Lord" was concerned with divorce (1 Cor 7:10–11); 3. Jesus had a last meal with his followers (1 Cor 11:24+); 4. He was crucified and buried (Gal. 3:1; 1 Cor 15:4); 5. Jesus' mission was to the Jews (Rm 15:8); 6. Jesus believed ministers of the gospel would be paid for that service: "The Lord directed those who proclaim the gospel to get their living from the gospel" (1 Cor 9:14); 7. Jesus had brothers (1 Cor 9:5); 8. James (Jacov) was one of Jesus' brothers (Gal 1:19); 9. Jesus had 12 special disciples (1 Cor 15:5); 10. Betrayal was part of Jesus' death (1 Cor 11:23); 11. Peter was a special follower to whom Jesus appeared (1 Cor 15:5); 12. Important followers of Jesus included James, Peter, and John "those reputed to be pillars" (Gal 2:9); 13. Paul sees Jesus as deriving from the root of Jesse (Rm 15:8).

PAUL'S POLITICAL CONTEXT

Unlike Jesus who was protesting the way the Herodian regime ran the Temple, Paul is entangled with tensions between Jews and Gentiles while relativizing

93

the significance of Roman rule. Scholars debate to what degree Paul has an anti-imperial agenda. For Paul, Jesus and his God are his primary concern; loyalty to Roman authority is secondary. Romans who are not in Christ are likely to be guided by unrighteousness (Rm 1). The wickedness of Romans 1 is not specifically distinguished from that of Greeks or Romans, but there is a condemnation of participating in the imperial cult of Caesar in Roman 1:23: "they became fools, and exchanged the glory of the immortal God for images resembling mortal man." The Roman empire does not appear to be a major factor in Paul's thinking, but he does say it will fade away. "For the present form of this world is passing away" (1 Cor 7:31). That world of sin and death is now being influenced by Christ and his Spirit in people who are initiating a new creation (Rm 8; 2 Cor 5; Gal 6). In the meantime he acknowledges that Roman authority expresses God's will (Rm 13). Paul's belief in the second coming allows for and facilitates subordination to unjust rulers; Roman rule is not ultimate in light of relationship with a liberating God.

There are subversive statements in his letters: "Yet among the mature we do impart wisdom, although it is not a wisdom of this age or of the rulers of this age, who are doomed to pass away" (1 Cor 2:6).

He blames the Romans for the death of Jesus: "we impart a secret and hidden wisdom of God, which God decreed before the ages for our glorification. None of the rulers of this age understood this; for if they had, they would not have crucified the Lord of glory" (1 Cor 2:8–9).

Paul considered the Roman regime as unrighteous. The world Paul describes in Romans 1:18–32 is one where God's sovereignty is unrecognized and was filled with "ungodliness and wickedness" (1:18). Elsewhere he describes his time as "the present evil age" (Gal 1:4). This was against Roman propaganda that said Rome was an example for the world. Paul's contemporary, Valerius Maximus (*Facta et dicta*, 6.5), claims that "Among all nations our society is the outstanding and clearest example" of righteousness (from Haaker in Ballentine under "Justice," Ballentine, Samuel, *The Oxford Encyclopedia of the Bible and Theology*, New York: Oxford University Press, 2015).

Though seeing Rome as unrighteous, he did not advocate overthrowing Roman rule. His "rulers of this age" comment puts Roman rule as subordinate to God's rule, while Rom 13 asserts Roman authority as expressive of God's rule. This idea is found in Proverbs: "By me [God] kings reign, and rulers decree what is just; by me princes rule, and nobles govern the earth" (Proverbs 8:15–16). Similar to Paul, Josephus wanted his Jewish contemporaries to see Roman authority as an extension of the authority of the God of the Jews: "O miserable creatures! are you so unmindful of those that used to assist you, that you will fight by your weapons and by your hands against the Romans? When did we ever conquer any other nation by such means? . . . hearken to me, that you may be informed how you fight not only against the Romans, but against God himself" (*Jewish Wars*, 5.9.4). Likewise, Paul wanted people to pay their taxes to Rome: "For the same reason you also pay taxes, for the authorities are ministers of God" (Rm 13:6).

Roman literature was written by elite members of society and applauded Roman rule and its stability:

> Time lay the foundation for the Roman State and, with the help of God, so combine and join together Fortune and Virtue that, by taking the peculiar qualities of each, he might construct for all mankind a Hearth, in truth both holy and beneficent, a steadfast cable, a principle abiding forever, "an anchorage from the swell and drift" . . . the continuous movement, drift, and change of all peoples remained without remedy, until such time as Rome acquired strength and growth, and had attached to herself not only the nations and peoples within her own borders, but also royal dominions of foreign peoples beyond the seas, and thus the affairs of this vast empire gained stability and security, since the supreme government, which never knew reverse, was brought within an orderly and single cycle of peace. (Plutarch, *Moralia*: "The Fortune of the Romans," 2)

Paul warns against "peace and security" that was part of Roman propaganda: "When people say, 'There is peace and security,' then sudden destruction will come upon them as travail comes upon a woman with child, and there will be no escape" (1 Th 5:3).

Despite general stability promoted in Roman propaganda, subjugated people did not enjoy the same peace as the rulers. Plutarch devotes an entire chapter of the *Moralia* to "Principles of Statecraft," thus acknowledging that not everyone under Roman rule was cooperative. In response to rebellion, Plutarch writes: "frequently differences arising from private affairs and offences pass thence into public life and throw the whole State into confusion. Therefore it behooves the statesman above all things to remedy or prevent these" (32).

There were numerous revolts in Palestine against Roman authority. Insecurity among Christians would be common as they were persecuted, taxed, and some were enslaved (e.g., Onesimus) by the Romans:

> Nero fastened the guilt [concerning the fire in Rome] and inflicted the most exquisite tortures on a class hated for their abominations, called Christians by the populace. . . . Mockery of every sort was added to their deaths. Covered with the skins of beasts, they were torn by dogs and perished, or were nailed to crosses, or were doomed to the flames and burnt, to serve as a nightly illumination, when daylight had expired. (Tacitus, *Annals*, 15)

Paul added to insecurity; as a Roman Jew he had persecuted Christians: "I persecuted the church of God violently and tried to destroy it" (Gal 1:11). Despite social insecurity Paul did not advocate overthrow of Roman rule.

CHRIST CRUCIFIED

The central understanding of Jesus for Paul is Christ crucified. This may be surprising as he did not follow Jesus prior to the crucifixion and participated in the persecution and murder of Christians. When writing to the Corinthians in the letter called 1 Corinthians, he says he came to Corinth knowing nothing but Christ crucified (1 Cor 2:2).

A focal point for Paul's preaching of Christ crucified is the problem of divisions within the community (1 Cor 1–4). The Corinthians were "puffed up one against another" (1 Cor 4:6, RSV) or taking "pride in one man over against another" (NIV). He holds up the example of Christ crucified to poke a hole in the inflated egos of those Corinthians who were elevating themselves based on association with particular spiritual teachers (1 Cor 1:11–17; 3:5–7, 18; 4:6+). Christ on the cross is an example of self-sacrifice, not of someone aspiring to wealth, status or power.

In several chapters in the body of the letter, Paul shows the implications of Christ crucified for solving problems and for handling life. In chapter 6 Paul counsels the Corinthians concerning lawsuits. He thinks they should settle matters among themselves rather than taking a community member to court. To sue a member of one's community will create division, and he wants unity. His remedy is to endure the injustice. "Why not rather be wronged? Why not rather be cheated?" (1 Cor 6:7). This profound challenge to ordinary reaction appears to be a reflection of Christ crucified who put up with mistreatment. I say "appears" because Paul does not reiterate the image of Christ on the cross in that chapter, but in chapter 4 he uses his own example reminding the Corinthians "of my way of life in Christ Jesus": "When we are cursed, we bless; when we are persecuted, we endure it; when we are slandered, we answer kindly" (1 Cor 4:12–13, 17). The goal is not suffering; the goal is unity, and the way is self-sacrifice for the sake of the community. This solution of enduring wrong is a particular solution to a particular problem 2000 years ago; it does not necessarily apply to all people in all times.

In chapters 8 and 10, Paul is responding to the question whether Christians may eat meat that has been offered in sacrifice to pagan gods. Though Paul agrees there are no other gods and that Christians are free from dietary laws, he counsels the Corinthians to be mindful of the impact of their example on others in the community who may not be as clear about monotheism and Christian freedom. For the sake of these less than enlightened members,

Paul asks people who are already aware of their freedom from dietary laws to refrain from exercising their right to eat any type of food they wish. This principle of self-sacrifice for the sake of others is the same one operating in the question of lawsuits. To help the Corinthians understand, Paul brings into focus his own behavior with regard to his rights in chapter 9. He says he has the right to be paid for his service, but he foregoes exercise of his right (9:13) so as to not burden the community.

Self-sacrifice for the sake of others, a reflection of Christ crucified applies to the case of the poor being humiliated in the celebration of the Eucharist: "Or do you despise the church of God and humiliate those who have nothing?" (11:22). The likely scenario was sharing of the ceremonial cup and breaking of the bread along with a real meal in which all participants brought food for others to share. A poor person who had nothing to contribute might feel embarrassed. Paul tells the Corinthians to change the way they celebrate the Eucharist by keeping the breaking of the bread and sharing of the cup but to leave the meal that answers to hunger at home (11:34). Change for the sake of others is Paul's recurring direction.

The last place in 1 Corinthians where self-sacrifice for the sake of the community comes into play, is in chapters 12 and 14 where the gift of speaking in tongues has caused some confusion. This is a method of affective prayer in which someone with childlikeness utters unintelligible syllables as a form of devotion to God. Paul is not against this type of prayer, but he prefers to use gifts that benefit others such as prophecy or teaching. He says speaking in tongues benefits the person praying rather than the community. In chapter 12, he affirms the principle of diversity. There is a variety of gifts which would preclude the use of one gift such as speaking in tongues to become a type of litmus test for the presence of the Spirit. In chapter 14 he proclaims, "I would rather speak five intelligible words to instruct others than ten thousand words in a tongue" (1 Cor 14:19). He is not denying the personal benefit of speaking in tongues, nor certainly the right to pray in this way, but he is asking the Corinthians to opt for the gifts and the behaviors that benefit the community. Self-sacrifice for the sake of others is the message of Paul that he associates with Christ crucified through much of this letter.

LAST ADAM: LIFE GIVING SPIRIT

In 1 Corinthians 15, Paul complains to the Corinthians that they are having difficulty believing in the resurrection of the dead. The Corinthians received and accepted Paul's preaching about the death and resurrection of Jesus: "the gospel I preached to you, which you received and on which you have taken your stand" (1 Cor 1:1). The problem Paul identifies in 15:12 is not the resurrection of Jesus which they accepted but the resurrection of the dead, the resurrection of anyone else. (This is similar to 1 Thessalonians 4, where Paul's readers were reminded that the dead would not miss out on the second coming.)

The resurrection of Jesus was misunderstood in some of the regions Paul travelled. In early Christian preaching, baptism meant "dying," as immersion into water brings death to those who do not have gills. Coming out of the water signified rising to newness of life. Dying and rising are symbolic terms meaning a turning away from former sinful living to new life in Christ. We have Pauline language that uses these terms freely: "having been buried with him in baptism and raised with him through your faith in the power of God, who raised him from the dead" (Colossians 2:12) and "made us alive with Christ even when we were dead in transgressions—it is by grace you have been saved" (Ephesians 2:5). These passages use past tense for death and present tense for resurrection.

This symbolic language was apparently taken literally by some, thus giving the idea that resurrection was a past event in the lives of believers: " . . . who have wandered away from the truth. They say that the resurrection has already taken place, and they destroy the faith of some" (2 Timothy 2:18). One source of misunderstanding of resurrection may be linked to taking literally the language of baptism.

This misunderstanding could have been reinforced by incipient Gnostic belief; the Gnostic texts succeed Pauline writing, but early Gnostics may have been influential in Paul's day. *The Gospel of Philip*, a 2nd-century collection of sayings of Gnostic origin (22 in http://gospelofthomas.nazirene.org /philip.htm also referred to as saying 97), says "Those who say, 'One will first die and then rise,' are in error. If one does not first receive the resurrection while one is still alive, one will receive nothing upon dying. This is the way they also speak of baptism, saying 'Great is baptism, for in receiving it one will live.'" Saying 22 says, "Those who say, 'The Lord died first and then rose,' are in error for he first rose and then died." (For a similar saying, see the *Gospel According to Thomas*, saying 51.) Here the experience of the Gnostic involving some kind of mystical illumination could be interpreted as resurrection.

Whether the understanding was of baptism as resurrection or as mystical illumination, neither deal with the real issue of death. Paul wants the Corinthians to see resurrection from the dead in real terms, not simply metaphorical or epistemological.

In the midst of his argument, Paul makes a contrast between the first Adam and the last Adam (1 Cor 15:22). Whether he is arguing against those influenced by Philo, a contemporary of Paul, by Gnostics, or by Rabbinic scholars is the subject of unresolved debate (see Hultgren, 343–370). Philo, using the two creations of Adam in Genesis (1:27 and 2:7), saw two Adams representing two moral tendencies in humans. "The one that was moulded is the more earthly mind, the one that was made the less material, having no part in perishable matter, endowed with a constitution of a purer and clearer kind" (Philo, *Allegorical Interpretation*, I.88). If God breathes his spirit into the human mind, a human being can rise above passion and know God. (Hultgren, 349). "This earthlike mind is in reality also corruptible, were not God to breathe into it a power of real life" (Philo, *Allegorical Interpretation*, I.32). Philo notwithstanding, Paul ascribes the gift of life to Christ. "'The first man Adam became a living being'; the last Adam, a life-giving spirit" (1 Cor 15:45). I am not suggesting any sort of borrowing here, but simply that the two Adams idea was in the air when Paul was writing. Paul's focus is on Christ as giver of life after death.

Gnostics also speculated about the inner and outer man, and Rabbinic discussion also included discourse on the two conceptions of humans in this world and the future world (Hultgren). The point Paul is making may answer to all of these influences. It is unclear if Paul is responding to these other voices or simply to his own experience of transformation through ongoing conversion (2 Cor 3:18).

Paul is saying life after death is not something built in to human nature, answering the Gnostic assumption of immortal soul. The image of the man of dust is not sufficient for resurrected life; the need is for a gift of the spirit of God for resurrection, thus agreeing with Philo for the need of the spirit of God, though going beyond Philo to say Christ is the life giver. Resurrection for Paul will involve a refashioning, coincidentally supporting rabbinic speculation about the refashioning in the world to come. For Paul, resurrection is a transforming gift through the mediation of Christ.

The first man was of the dust of the earth, the second man from heaven. As was the earthly man, so are those who are of the earth; and as is the man from heaven, so also are those who are of heaven. And just as we have borne the likeness of the earthly man, so shall we bear the likeness of the man from heaven. I declare to you, brothers, that flesh and blood cannot inherit the kingdom of God, nor does the perishable inherit the imperishable. (1 Cor 15:47–50)

FREEDOM AND THE LAW

Source of freedom is synonymous to "liberator," but liberator is currently associated with economic and social transformations which are difficult to relate to Paul. Paul, after all had a short view of history; "the time is short" (1 Cor 7:29). He did not principally deal with transformation of the social and economic orders. He did not even directly challenge the institution of slavery. He did, however, ask for money for the poor with a social justice principle: "Our desire is not that others might be relieved while you are hard pressed, but that there might be equality" (2 Cor 8:13). Had Paul lived within an expansive view of the future, he might well have engaged in a project to transform society's structures, and contemporary Christians can legitimately develop his ideas well beyond his historical limitations. When looking at Paul and freedom, however, his original meaning was tied to certain Jewish practices, namely kosher dietary law and circumcision.

Paul famously develops his thought about "freedom from the law" mainly in his letters to the Galatians and to the Romans. One can tie Jesus to Paul's breakthrough insight concerning human freedom. He writes in Romans, "Therefore, there is now no condemnation for those who are in Christ Jesus, because through Christ Jesus the law of the Spirit of life set me free from the law of sin and death" (Rm 8:1–2). Here Paul sees his freedom from efforts to secure his existence through obedience to laws as a result of harmonizing his life to his relationship with Christ.

Paul knew Jesus through an interior connection rather than through an encounter with the earthly Jesus. This relationship that sustained Paul through his life of tribulation is the source of his freedom from religious laws. Paul's rejection of obedience to law as source of guidance was supported by another source of guidance namely his relationship with the risen Christ. "For you did not receive a spirit that makes you a slave again to fear, but you received the Spirit of sonship. And by him we cry, 'Abba, Father.' The Spirit himself testifies with our spirit that we are God's children. Now if we are children, then we are heirs—heirs of God and co-heirs with Christ, if indeed we share in his sufferings in order that we may also share in his glory" (Rm 8:15–17).

Hardly anything about Paul's writing has received more attention than his discussion of freedom and law; a brief summary here will clarify a few points. First of all Paul was not against law either civil or religious. Paul was challenging the motivation behind obedience to religious law. His language was "justification" by faith not by law: "know that a man is not justified by observing the law, but by faith in Jesus Christ. So we, too, have put our faith in Christ Jesus that we may be justified by faith in Christ and not by observing the law, because by observing the law no one will be justified" (Gal 2:16; see also Rm 3:28 and Galatians chapter 3).

Remember Paul's original circumstance is one where he is preaching largely to Gentiles and explaining the importance or necessity of kosher dietary law and circumcision (especially circumcision of adults!) would have been challenging at least. When one considers the situation of preaching to an adult Gentile and then explaining the necessity of circumcision, that would in many cases be a deal breaker. Paul saw the relative unimportance of these practices and dropped them. He saw further into the dangers of religious law.

His language about law becomes progressively more negative from early letters to later letters. In 1 Cor 7:19, his view is positive where he counsels people to keep the commandments. At the same time, he is indifferent about circumcision. In Philippians he contrasts "righteousness of my own based on law but that which is through faith in Christ" (3:9). This contrast is not as negative as what he writes in 2 Corinthians: "The written code kills" (3:6). In Galatians, he argues, "All under law are under a curse" (3:10), including Jesus, who was cursed by the law (3:13). Deuteronomy contains a curse on all who hang on a tree (Dt 21:23). Paul's argument is, how can you Christians expect to find life in the law that cursed Jesus! Notice he argues against law generically, not just circumcision and kosher dietary law.

The Jewish law was added as a kind of custodian (Gal 3:24). In Romans, the law brings wrath (Romans 4:15); the law increases trespass: "The law was added so that the trespass might increase" (Rm 5:20). Paul's point is the grace of God outstrips human sinfulness, but he has very little that is positive to say about religious law.

He is not against moral living which in many cases is consistent with religious law. What Paul wants to emphasize is faith in God over faith in one's ability to keep religious rules.

People in relation to the God of the Bible are faced with high ideals and their own less than excellent and consistent performance. As Paul reminds the Romans, "all have sinned and fall short of the glory of God" (Rm 3:23). One way of handling this situation is through careful observance of religious rules: giving money to the poor, regular prayer, participation in religious services, kindness to those in need, and reading of the Scriptures. These good practices can serve to deepen conscious relationship with God or to distance oneself from God. If the motivation behind these religious activities is to handle God or to manage God, then observance can become an insulating blanket between oneself and God. If one does all of the good things prescribed by the religion, one might take refuge behind one's observance and think one has taken God off of one's case. This is to use religion to separate self from God. Paul intends relatedness to God to be primary; the word he uses is "faith." He wants people to depend upon God and God's favor over any human performance.

Paul aims to protect human freedom from the thinking that one can manage God by good works. "It is for freedom that Christ has set us free. Stand firm, then, and do not let yourselves be burdened again by a yoke of slavery" (Gal 5:1). Paul, at the same time, counsels good works, but these should spring from faith (Gal 5:6). Freedom is not an excuse for sinful behavior: "You, my brothers, were called to be free. But do not use your freedom to indulge the sinful nature; rather, serve one another in love" (Gal 5:13).

If Paul wants an ordered life, a morally upright life, he wants it to be motivated by love. "For in Christ Jesus neither circumcision nor uncircumcision has any value. The only thing that counts is faith expressing itself through love" (Gal 5:16). He does not use the word "motivation," but this text shows his concern is for what drives the good works. "Whatever does not proceed from faith is sin" (Rm 14:23). Faith expressed through love will lead to a morally good life. He is giving a critique of the motivation behind good works, not of good works themselves.

From his autobiographical statements it is clear Paul saw a connection to the Jesus of his mystical experience in all of this discussion of freedom. He found a freedom from his former way of life in which he was blameless before the law, while yet being a person willing to participate in the murder of Christians (see especially Philippians 3; Gal. 1:11+). Jesus the risen Christ was Paul's liberator; he found in him a transcendent source of guidance and recognized his former life of religious observance to have been off the track.

SOURCE OF UNITY

As already discussed above in the context of self-sacrifice for the sake of others in 1 Corinthians, and of spiritual gifts in 1 Corinthians 12–14, Paul believes each person's gifts should be put at the service of the community. Paul attempted to foster unity in his communities and used the imagery of body to depict the interplay of unity and diversity. "Just as each of us has one body with many members, and these members do not all have the same function, so in Christ we who are many form one body, and each member belongs to all the others. We have different gifts, according to the grace given us" (Rm 12:4–6). While both 1 Corinthians chapters 12 and 14 and Romans 12 use the term "body" to describe the relationship among community members, it is in the Pauline letters of Ephesians and Colossians that the term "head of the body" surfaces. "And God placed all things under his feet and appointed him to be head over everything for the church, which is his body, the fullness of him who fills everything in every way" (Eph 1:22–23; see also 5:23 and Col 1:18).

Unity between Jews and Gentiles was another concern for Paul especially in his Letter to the Romans. The sources of tension between Jews and Gentiles in Rome may not be completely transparent. The Letter to the Galatians shows they had different views concerning circumcision and diet (Gal 2). In Rome there may have been an additional irritant. As mentioned in the chapter on Mark's Gospel, Jews and Gentiles were persecuted by

Romans, and sometimes Romans did not distinguish between them. Jews and Gentiles were both described as practicing "*superstitio*," which was poison for the mind according to Cicero (*De Finibus*, I:18; see Tacitus, *Annals*, 15:44; Cicero, *Pro Flacco*, 28:67). Jews, including Jews who followed Jesus, were thrown out of Rome: "Paul left Athens and went to Corinth. There he met a Jew named Aquila, a native of Pontus, who had recently come from Italy with his wife Priscilla, because Claudius had ordered all Jews to leave Rome" (Acts 18:2). Aquila and Priscilla appear to have been Jewish Christians (see Acts 18:26; Rm 16:3). It is likely that synagogue attending Jewish Christians would have been more easily identified and uprooted by Claudius [49 CE], whereas Gentile Christians may have been less obvious to Roman authorities as the Gentile Christians would not have been frequenting synagogues. Whatever divided Jews and Gentiles in Rome, Paul in his Letter to the Romans (ch. 1–3) hammers home that Jews and Gentiles are in the same boat as sinners, and their only hope was Jesus. "There is no difference between Jew and Gentile, for all have sinned and fall short of the glory of God, and all are justified freely by his grace" (Rm 3:24). Jesus was the source of unity for both Jewish and Gentile Christians. "Therefore welcome one another as Christ has welcomed you, for the glory of God. For I tell you that Christ became a servant to the circumcised to show God's truthfulness, in order to confirm the promises given to the patriarchs, and in order that the Gentiles might glorify God for his mercy" (Rm 15:7–9).

REDEEMER

In several places Paul refers to Jesus as source of redemption. The most fertile text is Romans 3:24–25:

> They are justified by his grace as a gift, through the redemption (*apolytrōseos*) which is in Christ Jesus, whom God put forward as an expiation (*hilasterion*) by his blood, to be received by faith. This was to show God's righteousness, because in his divine forbearance he had passed over former sins. (Rm 3:24–25)

These words have generated an array of interpretations, some of which give strange notions of a God who punishes his Son or of a God who needs to be persuaded by His Son! I will offer an understanding that avoids those.

Paul takes words from the Hebrew contexts of 1) freeing a slave and 2) from animal sacrifice and applies them metaphorically to the death of Jesus.

1. *Apolytrōseos* is usually translated as redemption. In the Greek translation of the O.T. this referred to liberation of slaves. "If she does not

please her master, who has designated her for himself, then he shall let her be redeemed" (Ex 21:8 in the Septuagint). Liberation here is generally associated with payment or ransom. Jesus is not paying anyone; rather, he is doing all he can even to the point of risking his own life to liberate those who are oppressed.

2. "Expiation (*hilasterion*) by his blood" means what? *Hilasterion* might well be translated as "mercy seat" as it is in Heb 9:5 and numerous times in the Septuagint (Ex 25:17, 18, 19, 20, 21, 22; 31:7; 35:12; 37:6, 8, 9; Lev 16:2, 13, 14, 15, Nu 7:89; Ezk 43:14, 17, 20; Am 9:1). Paul, who uses the term only once, is using the word metaphorically by taking a term out of the Hebrew setting of animal sacrifice and applying it to the death of Jesus. Blood in O.T. was a cleansing agent that could undo the polluting effect of sin: "For the life of the flesh is in the blood; and I have given it to you for making atonement for your lives on the altar; for, as life, it is the blood that makes atonement" (Lev 17:11). Blood was sprinkled on the altar or mercy seat to cleanse it, as it had been polluted by sinfulness: " . . . and he shall take some of the blood of the bull, and sprinkle it with his finger on the front of the mercy seat, and before the mercy seat he shall sprinkle the blood with his finger seven times "(Lev 16:14). For more on this see Finlan, Stephen, *Problems with Atonement: The Origins of, and Controversy about, the Atonement Doctrine* (Collegeville MN: Liturgical Press, 2005), ch. 1–2. The animals were sacrificed for this purpose of getting the blood out of the animal to neutralize sin by sprinkling the blood on the altar; the animals were not punished! Later theologians fancifully and erroneously wrote that Jesus was punished for the sins of humanity!

Paul combines payment for liberation and cleansing in these two lines of Romans 3:24–25. The "mercy seat" (*hilasterion* translates the Hebrew *kapporeth*) was the place that was sprinkled with blood to cleanse the Temple.

How can Jesus be understood metaphorically as the "mercy seat?" Though some would understand sprinkling blood as a kind of magic or cultic detergent, others would have used the ritual to express repentance. Hebrew people wanting to dissociate themselves from their sins took their sins to the priest who in turn took their sins to the mercy seat, see Zohar, Noam, "Repentance and Purification" *JBL* 107, no. 4 (1988): 614–615. Obviously sins are not objects that can be transferred. What is transferred? People transfer their hope, their aspirations, their intentions to God. People hoped that God would mercifully receive their interior commitment and forgive their sins. In this implied repentance is redemption. Jesus' life and teaching manifested God's intention to forgive, so people hoped that Jesus would represent them before the throne of God.

There is no implication of God punishing Jesus or Jesus changing God's mind. Those thoughts project God to be less than the best human being.

LORD

Paul calls Jesus Lord. This title carries more weight than simply a title of respect as one would find in the disciples' response to Jesus. In the arrest of Jesus for example in Luke, Jesus is deferentially asked, "Lord, should we strike with our swords?" (22:49).

Paul uses the word "Lord" in a higher sense. Lord, as explained above in the chapter on John's Gospel, is a substitute for the word Yahweh in the Hebrew Scriptures. In place of YHWH, Jewish readers were accustomed to use *Adonai*, Lord. The shift in meaning from I Am or He Who Is, expressing the unique existence of God became the presence of the ruler of heaven and earth. In the Septuagint, YHWH became Lord, *kurios*. Isaiah uses "Lord" in the sense of *Adonai*: "For thus says the LORD, The creator of the heavens, who is God, The designer and maker of the earth who established it, Not as an empty waste did he create it, but designing it to be lived in: I am the LORD, and there is no other" (Is 45:18 NABRE). The text continues with words filled with the sense of supreme authority: "To me every knee shall bend; by me every tongue shall swear" (23). This is the same language Paul uses in Philippians: "that at the name of Jesus every knee should bend, of those in heaven and on earth and under the earth, and every tongue confess that Jesus Christ is Lord" (Philippians 2:10–11). The same special meaning of Lord as used by the prophet Joel shows up in Paul. "Everyone who calls on the name of the Lord will be saved" (Joel 2:32). Paul quotes this passage and applies it to Jesus (For fuller discussion of this see Parke-Taylor 97+) showing his own identification of Jesus with the Lord of salvation in the Hebrew Bible.

> That if you confess with your mouth, "Jesus is Lord," and believe in your heart that God raised him from the dead, you will be saved. For it is with your heart that you believe and are justified, and it is with your mouth that you confess and are saved. As the Scripture says, "Anyone who trusts in him will never be put to shame." For there is no difference between Jew and Gentile—the same Lord is Lord of all and richly blesses all who call on him, for, "Everyone who calls on the name of the Lord will be saved." (Rm 10:9–13)

CHRIST IS THE HEAD OF EVERY MAN?

Paul calls Jesus the head of every man. This is hardly a portrait of Jesus as much as it is a reflection of first century patriarchal thinking. Paul writes "But I want you to realize that the head of every man is Christ, and the head of the woman is man, and the head of Christ is God" (1 Cor 11:3). Paul uses the word *andros* meaning male rather than the generic *anthropos*. He gives a hierarchy in which God is at the top, followed by Jesus, followed by males, and then females at the bottom of the staircase. Paul is trying to keep veils on women and men without head coverings. A benign reading of this is in his communities women had some authority especially in household churches. (See Rom 16:7; Junia is a female apostle.) Within houses women did not need to be veiled. When the Pauline churches expanded beyond houses, women who were accustomed to participating and leading Christian ritual without veils went out of doors without head covering, and this upset some. Paul is trying to avoid conflict concerning the appearance of women and men, and he theologizes about it. He refers to the creation of Eve in Gen 2 out of a rib of Adam, making woman derivative. The obvious problem for contemporary readers with Paul's hierarchy is in interpreting every word Paul utters as having universal applicability. Paul was dealing as best he could with local problems, some of which have universal value, and some do not. (For more on this, see Capper, 123–151, or 5 and 6 digital version http://www.ntgateway .com/gospel-and-acts/luke-and-acts/articles. There are many good treatments of Paul on women, but they are beyond the scope of this guide.)

Aside from this gender related hierarchical view, Paul's presentation of Jesus is a source of unity, freedom, and life. The cross of Christ gives concreteness to Paul's integration of the wisdom from the risen Christ into daily life. For Paul the risen Christ is one with the Lord of heaven and earth, the Lord known to the Hebrew prophets.

Appendix

HISTORICAL BACKGROUND TO
THE NEW TESTAMENT

For centuries the Jewish people had been dominated by a variety of nations, among them Assyria, Babylon, Persia, Greece, and Rome. Josephus refers to this as he ends one of his works *The Antiquities* with the following summation:

> These Antiquities contain what hath been delivered down to us from the original creation of man, until the twelfth year of the reign of Nero, as to what hath befallen the Jews, as well in Egypt as in Syria and in Palestine, and what we have suffered from the Assyrians and Babylonians, and what afflictions the Persians and Macedonians, and after them the Romans, have brought upon us; for I think I may say that I have composed this history with sufficient accuracy in all things. (Josephus, *Antiquities*, 20.11.2)

A few highlights from the history of the Jews will help to contextualize the New Testament.

Babylonian Captivity (586–537 BCE)

Under Babylonian King Nebuchadnezzar the Hebrew people in Israel suffered destruction of their Temple in Jerusalem (Solomon's Temple), and many were taken into exile in Babylon. "Thus says the LORD of hosts, the God of Israel, to all the exiles whom I have sent into exile from Jerusalem to Babylon . . . because they did not heed my words, says the Lord, which I persistently sent to you by my servants the prophets, but you would not listen, says the Lord" (Jer 29:4, 19). Here Jeremiah blamed his own people for their suffering; this interpretation has God punishing them for disobedience. In their period of captivity in Babylon the Hebrew people had a religion without a Temple, and they consequently focused more on texts and morality. Here is where they became a people of the Book, and numerous books of the Bible were written. In 538 BCE, they were freed by Cyrus the Persian from the Babylonians and allowed to return to their homeland but under Persian rule.

Persian Period (538–336 BCE)

Since they had been held in a foreign land, the Jews felt a need to retain their identity through their religious traditions. They formulated literature to record these traditions; this became a period of intense literary output when additional books of the Bible were produced. They began to reconstruct the Temple now known as the "Second Temple." Later in the Roman period, this Temple was refurbished and expanded by Herod.

Hellenistic Period (336–63 BCE)

Alexander the Great (an educated imperialist who had studied under Aristotle) conquered the eastern Mediterranean region and the Middle East. His motives were undoubtedly mixed, and Plutarch later ascribed to him an intention to civilize this region:

> But if you examine the results of Alexander's instruction, you will see that he educated the Hyrcanians to respect the marriage bond, and taught the Arachosians to till the soil, and persuaded the Sogdians to support their parents, not to kill them, and the Persians to revere their mothers and not to take them in wedlock. O wondrous power of Philosophic Instruction, that brought the Indians to worship Greek gods, and the Scythians to bury their dead, not to devour them! . . . But when Alexander was civilizing Asia, Homer was commonly read, and the children of the Persians, of the Susianians, and of the Gedrosians learned to chant the tragedies of Sophocles and Euripides. And although Socrates, when tried on the charge of introducing foreign deities, lost his cause to the informers who infested Athens, yet through Alexander Bactria and the Caucasus learned to revere the gods of the Greeks . . . Alexander established more than seventy cities among savage tribes, and sowed all Asia with Grecian magistracies, and thus overcame its uncivilized and brutish manner of living. Although few of us read Plato's Laws, yet hundreds of thousands have made use of Alexander's laws, and continue to use them. Those who were vanquished by Alexander are happier than those who escaped his hand; for these had no one to put an end to the wretchedness of their existence, while the victor compelled those others to lead a happy life. . . . Alexander's new subjects would not have been civilized, had they not been vanquished. . . . If, then, philosophers take the greatest pride in civilizing and rendering adaptable the intractable and untutored elements in human character, and if Alexander has been shown to have changed the savage

natures of countless tribes, it is with good reason that he should be regarded as a very great philosopher. (*Moralia*, 328c–329a) [Plutarch died in 120 CE]

He united the area through Greek culture, language, and money, hence facilitating the residents' geographical mobility.

This mobility, however, offered a new challenge to the self-understanding of citizens. People explored religions and philosophies to gain a sense of identity and some guidance and stability. Ethical philosophies such as Epicureanism, Stoicism, and Neo-Platonism offered help for people. Astrology became popular; mystery cults proliferated; Hellenistic Judaism developed; into this climate Christianity eventually emerged.

Jewish literature makes few references to Alexander. Josephus refers to him being welcomed into Jerusalem by many Judeans in Jerusalem. The high priest had originally been afraid but was reassured in a dream and thus went out to meet Alexander with respect. Alexander also had a dream, and in it the God worshipped by the Jews would give him victory over the Persians:

> That God who hath honored him with his high priesthood; for I saw this very person in a dream, in this very habit, when I was at Dios in Macedonia, who, when I was considering with myself how I might obtain the dominion of Asia, exhorted me to make no delay, but boldly to pass over the sea thither, for that he would conduct my army, and would give me the dominion over the Persians. (Josephus, *Antiquities*, 11.8, 4–6)

Alexander met the high priest and his entourage with respect, and Alexander offered sacrifice. The high priest in turn asked Alexander to allow Jews to follow their laws and not pay tribute to Alexander, which he granted. Many Jews joined Alexander's army to fight against the Persians.

> When he went up into the temple, he offered sacrifice to God, according to the high priest's direction, and magnificently treated both the high priest and the priests. And when the Book of Daniel was showed him wherein Daniel declared that one of the Greeks should destroy the empire of the Persians, he supposed that himself was the person intended. And as he was then glad, he dismissed the multitude for the present; but the next day he called them to him, and bid them ask what favors they pleased of him; whereupon the high priest desired that they might enjoy the laws of their forefathers, and might pay no tribute on the seventh year. He granted all they desired. And when they entreated him that he would permit the Jews in Babylon and Media to enjoy their own laws also, he willingly promised to do hereafter what they desired. And when he said to the multitude, that if any of them would enlist themselves in his army, on this condition, that they should continue under the laws of their forefathers, and live according to them, he was willing to take them with him, many were ready to accompany him in his wars. (Josephus, *Antiquities*, 11.8, 4–6)

However fantastic this story (dreams apparently had more weight in those days), there may be kernels of truth suggesting Jewish cooperation with Alexander.

With Alexander's death, his empire was divided into three kingdoms ruled by Hellenistic kings, who spawned dynasties. The Ptolemies ruled Egypt; the Seleucids ruled Lebanon, Syria, and Israel; the Antigonids ruled Greece until all three were conquered by the Romans.

Jewish Independence

Seleucid ruler Antiochus IV wanted to Hellenize the Jews and went so far as to attempt to dedicate the Temple in Jerusalem to Zeus. Tacitus refers to this time in history: "King Antiochus strove to destroy the national superstition and to introduce Greek civilization but was prevented by his war with the Parthians from at all improving this vilest of nations" (Tacitus, *Histories*, 5.8). 2 Maccabees describes this situation:

> When news of what had happened reached the king, he took it to mean that Judea was in revolt. So, raging inwardly, he left Egypt and took the city by storm And he commanded his soldiers to cut down relentlessly every one they met and to slay those who went into the houses. Then there was killing of young and old, destruction of boys, women, and children, and slaughter of virgins and infants. Within the total of three days eighty thousand were destroyed, forty thousand in hand-to-hand fighting; and as many were sold into slavery as were slain.
>
> Not content with this, Antiochus dared to enter the most holy temple in all the world, guided by Menelaus, who had become a traitor both to the laws and to his country. He took the holy vessels with his polluted hands, and swept away with profane hands the votive offerings which other kings had made to enhance the glory and honor of the place. Antiochus was elated in spirit, and did not perceive that the Lord was angered for a little while because of the sins of those who dwelt in the city, and that therefore he was disregarding the holy place. (2 Macc 5:11–17)
>
> Not long after this, the king sent an Athenian senator to compel the Jews to forsake the laws of their fathers and cease to live by the laws of God, and also to pollute the temple in Jerusalem and call it the temple of Olympian Zeus, and to call the one in Gerizim the temple of Zeus the Friend of Strangers, as did the people who dwelt in that place.
>
> Harsh and utterly grievous was the onslaught of evil. For the temple was filled with debauchery and reveling by the Gentiles, who dallied with harlots and had intercourse with women within the sacred precincts, and besides brought in things for sacrifice that were unfit. The altar was covered with abominable offerings which were forbidden by the laws. A man could neither keep the Sabbath, nor observe the feasts of his fathers, nor so much as confess himself to be a Jew.

On the monthly celebration of the king's birthday, the Jews were taken, under bitter constraint, to partake of the sacrifices; and when the feast of Dionysus came, they were compelled to walk in the procession in honor of Dionysus, wearing wreaths of ivy. At the suggestion of Ptolemy, a decree was issued to the neighboring Greek cities, that they should adopt the same policy toward the Jews and make them partake of the sacrifices, and should slay those who did not choose to change over to Greek customs. One could see, therefore, the misery that had come upon them. For example, two women were brought in for having circumcised their children. These women they publicly paraded about the city, with their babies hung at their breasts, then hurled them down headlong from the wall. (2 Macc 6:1–10)

The Greek desecration of the Temple was especially inflammatory as this was the main and for a long time the only Temple the Jews had; it was the place where sacrifices were made. (Josephus has several historical references to another Jewish temple called Temple of Onias, a Jewish high priest, in Egypt that could have functioned for more than 200 years. Josephus cites this temple in his *Antiquities* 13:32 and *Jewish Wars* 7:10+.) The Jerusalem Temple was the holiest place for the Jews; they turned and faced the Temple in Jerusalem from whatever place they were engaging in prayer. This Temple was dedicated to their one God which was defiled by Antiochus IV.

In the name of unity, Antiochus wanted to eliminate some Jewish practices. 1 Maccabees recounts:

> Then the king wrote to his whole kingdom that all should be one people, and that each should give up his customs to forbid burnt offerings and sacrifices and drink offerings in the sanctuary, to profane sabbaths and feasts, to defile the sanctuary and the priests, to build altars and sacred precincts and shrines for idols, to sacrifice swine and unclean animals, and to leave their sons uncircumcised. They were to make themselves abominable by everything unclean and profane, so that they should forget the law and change all the ordinances. And whoever does not obey the command of the king shall die . . . they erected a desolating sacrilege upon the altar of burnt offering. They also built altars in the surrounding cities of Judah. (1 Macc 1:41–50, 54)

Josephus also acknowledges desecration of the Temple by Antiochus with similar details. (See Josephus, *Antiquities*, 12.3–4.)

In addition to this religious persecution, resentment had been brewing, especially over taxation by Greeks who needed money to fight Romans. Some Judeans, led by Judah Maccabi of the Hasmonean family, revolted. (Judah was nicknamed Maccabi, which meant "the Hammer.") The revolt began around 167 BCE, and by 164 the Temple was cleansed. Jewish independence was secured by 142 BCE. Contemporary Jews commemorate this victory with the Feast of Hanukkah which marks the rededication of the Temple. Jewish independence lasted until the Romans marched into Jerusalem in 63 BCE, beginning the Roman Period.

Roman Period

As Roman invasion approached, the Hasmonean brothers Hyrcanus and Aristobulus were contesting for power over Judea. They called upon Rome to acquire power:

> Ambassadors came to him [Pompey], both from Aristobulus and Hyrcanus, and both desired he would assist them. And when both of them promised to give him money, Aristobulus four hundred talents, and Hyrcanus no less, he accepted of Aristobulus's promise, for he was rich, and had a great soul, and desired to obtain nothing but what was moderate; whereas the other was poor, and tenacious, and made incredible promises in hopes of greater advantages. (Josephus, *Antiquities*, 14.2.3; also ch.3)

The Roman general Pompey dominated both Hasmonean brothers and took control of Judea in 63 BCE. "Now we lost our liberty, and became subject to the Romans. . . . Moreover, the Romans exacted of us, in a little time, above ten thousand talents; and the royal authority, which was a dignity formerly bestowed on those that were high priests, by the right of their family" (Josephus, *Antiquities*, 14.4.5). Pompey allowed Hyrcanus to remain high priest. (Pompey then had to contend with Julius Caesar for power over the Roman empire.)

Roman rule included taxation. "Pompey . . . made Hyrcanus high priest . . . and laid a tribute upon the country, and upon Jerusalem itself" (Josephus, *Wars*, 1.7.6). This "tribute" consisted of one-fourth of what farmers in "Judea" produced annually to be paid every second year:

> Caius Caesar [=Julius], imperator the second time, hath ordained, That all the country of the Jews, excepting Joppa, do pay a tribute yearly for the city Jerusalem, excepting the seventh, which they call the sabbatical year, because thereon they neither receive the fruits of their trees, nor do they sow their land; and that they pay their tribute in Sidon on the second year [of that sabbatical period], the fourth part of what was sown: and besides this, they are to pay the same tithes to Hyrcanus and his sons which they paid to their forefathers. (Josephus, *Antiquities*, 14.10.6)
>
> THERE, was at this time a mighty war raised among the Romans upon the sudden and treacherous slaughter of Caesar by Cassius and Brutus, after he had held the government for three years and seven months . . . Cassius came into

Syria, . . . and went about exacting tribute of the cities, and demanding their money to such a degree as they were not able to bear . . .

So he gave command that the Jews should bring in seven hundred talents. . . . Now Herod, in the first place, mitigated the passion of Cassius, by bringing his share out of Galilee, which was a hundred talents, on which account he was in the highest favor with him. (Josephus, *Wars*, 1.11.1–2)

But when Herod was informed of this insurrection [in Galilee], he came to the assistance of the country immediately, and destroyed a great number of the seditions, and raised the sieges of all those fortresses they had besieged; he also exacted the tribute of a hundred talents of his enemies, as a penalty for the mutations they had made in the country. (*Wars*, 1.16.5)

Anti-taxation sentiment was later fueled by religious nationalism:

NOW Cyrenius, a Roman senator . . . came at this time into Syria, with a few others, being sent by Caesar to be a judge of that nation, and to take an account of their substance. . . . Cyrenius came himself into Judea, which was now added to the province of Syria, to take an account of their substance, and to dispose of Archelaus's money; but the Jews, although at the beginning they took the report of a taxation heinously, yet did they leave off any further opposition to it, by the persuasion of Joazar, who was the son of Beethus, and high priest; so they, being over-persuaded by Joazar's words, gave an account of their estates, without any dispute about it. Yet was there one Judas, a Gaulonite, of a city whose name was Gamala, who, taking with him Sadduc, a Pharisee, became zealous to draw them to a revolt, who both said that this taxation was no better than an introduction to slavery, and exhorted the nation to assert their liberty. (Josephus, *Antiquities*, 18.1.1; cf. Luke 2:1–2)

But of the fourth sect of Jewish philosophy, Judas the Galilean was the author. These men agree in all other things with the Pharisaic notions; but they have an inviolable attachment to liberty, and say that God is to be their only Ruler and Lord. (Josephus, *Antiquities*, 1.6)

Hyrcanus (Hasmonean leader) had been an official ally of Pompey, but Antipater now convinced Hyrcanus to switch sides and declare his allegiance to Julius Caesar. They then committed over 3,000 Jewish soldiers to invade Egypt. "Antipater, who managed the Jewish affairs, became very useful to Caesar when he made war against Egypt, and that by the order of Hyrcanus; . . . Antipater came to him, conducting three thousand of the Jews, armed men" (Josephus, *Antiquities*, 14.8). Why fight alongside Julius Caesar's troops? Sharon suggests, "It was the best way of getting on Caesar's good side after they had been allied . . . with his enemy Pompey" (Sharon, Nadav, *Judea under Roman Domination*, SBL 2017, 123). Julius Caesar gave the real power to Antipater, the Idumean (non-Judean, convert to Judaism), a rich person with political power in Idumea and supporter of Hyrcanus.

Antipater went on to support Gabinus who was a Roman ally of Pompey (see *Antiquities*, 14.1; 5.1). After the death of Pompey, Antipater supported Julius Caesar (*Antiquities*, 8.1).

The kingdom of Edom was conquered by the Nabataeans, and the western part became the independent kingdom of Idumea. The Idumeans had their own religion and were often enemies of the Jews. The Judean and Hasmonean king Hyrcanus had conquered Idumea. Hyrcanus forced the men of Idumea to be circumcised and to obey Jewish laws; this is the land from which Antipater, father of Herod, came.

> Hyrcanus . . . subdued all the Idumeans; and permitted them to stay in that country, if they would circumcise their genitals, and make use of the laws of the Jews; and they were so desirous of living in the country of their forefathers, that they submitted to the use of circumcision, and of the rest of the Jewish ways of living; at which time therefore this befell them, that they were hereafter no other than Jews. (Josephus, *Antiquities*, 13.9)

Antipater, friend of Hyrcanus, was also Idumean; how Jewish he was, is debatable: "Antipater was of the stock of the principal Jews who came out of Babylon into Judea; but that assertion of his was to gratify Herod, who was his son, and who, by certain revolutions of fortune, came afterward to be king of the Jews" (Josephus, *Antiquities*, 14.1.3). Herod had been made tetrarch and later king in part because Herod offered Mark Antony money: "Because Herod offered him money to make him king, as he had formerly given it him to make him tetrarch" (*Antiquities*, 14.14.4).

King Herod engaged in massive building campaigns including reconstructing, repairing, and expanding of the Temple in Jerusalem: "Herod . . . undertook a very great work, that is, to build of himself the temple of God, and make it larger in compass, and to raise it to a most magnificent altitude" (*Antiquities*, 15.11).

At the same time, according to Josephus, Herod as a dictator was hated:

> At which time Herod released to his subjects the third part of their taxes, under pretense indeed of relieving them, after the dearth they had had; but the main reason was, to recover their good-will, which he now wanted; for they were uneasy at him, because of the innovations he had introduced in their practices, of the dissolution of their religion, and of the disuse of their own customs; and the people everywhere talked against him, like those that were still more provoked and disturbed at his procedure; against which discontents he greatly guarded himself, and took away the opportunities they might have to disturb him, and enjoined them to be always at work; nor did he permit the citizens either to meet together, or to walk or eat together, but watched everything they did, and when any were caught, they were severely punished; and many there were who were

brought to the citadel Hyrcania, both openly and secretly, and were there put to death; and there were spies set everywhere, both in the city and in the roads, who watched those that met together; nay, it is reported that he did not himself neglect this part of caution, but that he would oftentimes himself take the habit of a private man, and mix among the multitude, in the night time, and make trial what opinion they had of his government: and as for those that could no way be reduced to acquiesce under his scheme of government, he prosecuted them all manner of ways; but for the rest of the multitude, he required that they should be obliged to take an oath of fidelity to him, and at the same time compelled them to swear that they would bear him good-will, and continue certainly so to do, in his management of the government; and indeed a great part of them, either to please him, or out of fear of him, yielded to what he required of them; but for such as were of a more open and generous disposition, and had indignation at the force he used to them, he by one means or other made away, with them. (*Antiquities*, 15.10.4)

Josephus chronicles numerous uprisings when King Herod had died. (See Josephus, *Wars*, 2.1+.) With the death of King Herod there was uncertainty about leadership. His son Archelaus wanted and needed Caesar Augustus to appoint him as king, but his brother Antipas was a rival (*Wars*, 2.2). Archelaus violently put down an insurrection in Jerusalem around the feast of Passover. This bloodshed was used against Archelaus by other sons, Antipater and Antipas. While Caesar Augustus was considering the accusations and thinking about who should succeed King Herod, there were several Jewish uprisings against the Romans (*Wars*, 2.3). A couple of these were led by men who proclaimed themselves as king (*Wars*, 2.4). A man named Simon "put a diadem upon his own head" (*Wars*, 2.4.2). Another was "a certain shepherd ventured to set himself up for a king; he was called Athrongeus" (*Wars*, 2.4.3). A shepherd who makes himself king would surely bring to the minds of some the memory of king David, whose descendants would be messiahs. All of this would have likely been known and remembered by Jesus' family, to Jesus, and to Gospel writers. Other Jews testified to Caesar against Archelaus, and Caesar limited Archelaus' authority:

So Caesar, after he had heard both sides, . . . a few days afterward, he gave the one half of Herod's kingdom to Archelaus, by the name of Ethnarch, and promised to make him king also afterward, if he rendered himself worthy of that dignity. But as to the other half, he divided it into two tetrarchies, and gave them to two other sons of Herod, the one of them to Philip, and the other to that Antipas who contested the kingdom with Archelaus. (*Wars*, 2.6.3; see also Horsley, *Jesus and the Politics of Roman Palestine*, 39, 59)

Archelaus treated both Jews and Samaritans "barbarously," and he was banished to Vienna (*Wars*, 2.7.3). As a result of Archelaus' poor leadership Augustus removed him. "Cyrenius came himself into Judea, which was now added to the province of Syria, to take an account of their substance, and to dispose of Archelaus's money." Judea was then under direct Roman rule as part of Syria (*Antiquities*, 18.1.1).

The references above to taxation heighten the need for some focus on poverty at the time of Jesus in Israel. For a good discussion of this, see Häkkinen, Sakari, "Poverty in the First-Century Galilee," *HTS*, 72, no. 4 (2016). The Gospels are written about times when Jesus and his followers have been controlled by the religious elite and by the Herodian regime. Herod and his offspring intensified the economic pressure on the local population in part as a result of his building campaign. Many inhabitants were subsistence farmers whose survival depended upon the quality of the harvest; when the crops failed these farmers were driven into debt and were at the mercy of money lenders. Foreclosure forced the unfortunate into becoming tenant farmers.

Not only were the Herodians predatory, but there is also evidence that priestly aristocrats could rightly be accused of similar greed: "Boldness that had seized on the high priests, that they had the hardiness to send their servants into the threshing-floors, to take away those tithes that were due to the priests, insomuch that it so fell out that the poorest sort of the priests died for want. To this degree did the violence of the seditious prevail over all right and justice" (Josephus, *Antiquities*, 20.8.7; also Horsley, *Jesus and the Politics of Roman Palestine*, 110). The Galileans at the time of Herod the Great had a threefold taxation system: tribute to Rome, taxes to Herod, and tithes and offerings to the Temple and priesthood (Häkkinen).

Foreign occupation and resistance movements provide a matrix for presenting Jesus' mission:

1. Conquest by the Roman general Pompey [63 BCE] unleashed decades of suffering upon the people living in Galilee and Judea. "Cassius [c. 43 BCE] had fled into that province, and when he had taken possession of the same, he made a hasty march into Judea; and, upon his taking Taricheae [Magdala on the Sea of Galilee], he carried thirty thousand Jews into slavery" (Jospehus, *Wars*, 1.8.9).
2. Divided loyalties as Hasmoneans and Herodians were vying for control, and many were killed. "When Herod had fought against these in the avenues of Judea, he was conqueror in the battle, and drove away Antigonus (a Hasmonean), and returned to Jerusalem, beloved by everybody for the glorious action he had done; for those who did not before favor him did join themselves to him now, because of his marriage into the family of Hyrcanus" (*Wars*, 1.12.3). "Herod . . . attacked

and slew many of the people, till one party made incursions on the other by turns, day by day, in the way of ambushes, and slaughters were made continually among them" (*Wars*, 1.13.2).

3. Herod, though loved by some at first, was hated as a tyrant: "The people everywhere talked against him" (Josephus, *Antiquities*, 15.10.4).

4. Around the death of Herod [c. 4 BCE] some pious Jews took down the golden eagle from the Temple wall in Jerusalem: " . . . a certain popular sedition . . . when these men were informed that the king was wearing away with melancholy, and with a distemper. . . . Now the king had put up a golden eagle over the great gate of the temple, which these learned men exhorted them to cut down; and told them, that if there should any danger arise, it was a glorious thing to die for the laws of their country; because that the soul was immortal, and that an eternal enjoyment of happiness did await such as died on that account" (*Wars*, 1.33.2).

5. The men who took down the golden eagle (mounted under the direction of King Herod) were killed; King Herod died, and people revolted:

And indeed, at the feast of unleavened bread, which was now at hand, and is by the Jews called the Passover, and used to be celebrated with a great number of sacrifices, an innumerable multitude of the people came out of the country to worship; some of these stood in the temple bewailing the Rabbins [that had been put to death], and procured their sustenance by begging, in order to support their sedition. At this Archelaus (Herod's son) was affrighted, and privately sent a tribune, with his cohort of soldiers, upon them, before the disease should spread over the whole multitude, and gave orders that they should constrain those that began the tumult, by force, to be quiet. At these the whole multitude were irritated, and threw stones at many of the soldiers, and killed them; but the tribune fled away wounded, and had much ado to escape so . . . Archelaus . . . sent his whole army upon them . . . destroyed about three thousand of them; but the rest of the multitude were dispersed upon the adjoining mountains. (Josephus, *Wars*, 2.1.3) [Archelaus: c. 23 BCE–18 CE]

6. After Jesus, when the war against the Romans began in 66 CE, Josephus indicates the resentment was associated with debt:

The others then set fire to the house of Ananias the high priest, and to the palaces of Agrippa and Bernice; after which they carried the fire to the place where the archives were reposited, and made haste to burn the contracts belonging to their creditors, and thereby to dissolve their obligations for paying their debts; and this was done in order to gain the multitude of those who had been debtors, and that they might persuade the poorer sort to join in their insurrection with safety against the more wealthy; so the keepers of the records fled away, and the rest set fire to them. And when they had thus burnt down the nerves of the city, they fell upon their enemies; at which time some of the men of power, and of the high priests, went into the vaults underground, and concealed themselves, while others fled with the king's soldiers to the upper palace, and shut the gates immediately; among whom were Ananias the high priest, and the ambassadors that had been sent to Agrippa. (*Wars*, 2.17.6)

Summary

1. Greek rule: Seleucid ruler: Antiochus IV who desecrated the Jerusalem Temple
2. Jewish self-rule (Hasmonean period). Maccabean revolt: Judah Maccabi (Judas Maccabeas) of the Hasmonean family: rededicated the Temple around 164 BCE.
3. Roman Period: 63 BCE–479 CE (approximate) 63 BCE Roman conquest by Pompey: "The occasions of this misery which came upon Jerusalem were Hyrcanus and Aristobulus, by raising a sedition one against the other; for now we lost our liberty, and became subject to the Romans" (Josephus, *Antiquities*, 14.4.5). This ended Hasmonean rule. Roman rule established in Israel with Antipater as procurator of Judea; he was father of Herod (37–4 BCE) client king of the Jews. Herod's offspring continued to rule after his death.

Consider the society in which Jesus lived: It was a theocracy controlled by a hated dictator, a puppet of the Roman empire, as well as by religious enthusiasts. "These Pharisees . . . bound and loosed [men] at their pleasure" (Josephus, *Wars*, 11.5.2). "These [Pharisees] have so great a power over the multitude, that when they say anything against the king, or against the high priest, they are presently believed" (Josephus, *Antiquities*, 13.10.5–6).

Decades before and after Jesus, there were numerous prophetic and messianic peasant uprisings against the religious elites (scribes, Sadducees, Pharisees), the Herodians, and the Romans (Josephus, *Antiquities*, 18.8; Josephus, *Wars*, 2.1.3; 2.12.1; 2.8.1; 2.13.4–5; 2.19.2; 4.9; 7.5.6; Acts 5:36; see Horsley, ch. 1, in Janz, *A Peoples History of Christianity*, vol. 1). Jesus' actions are part of this general tension, yet he does not advocate violence. Jesus was apparently calling people to renew their covenant with God which implied keeping commandments (Mark 7:8–13; 10:19; 14:24).

Bibliography

"2 Baruch." http://www.earlyjewishwritings.com/2baruch.html.

"4 Ezra." https://www.scribd.com/doc/2019085/4-Ezra-Revised-English.

Allison, Dale. *Constructing Jesus.* Baker, 2010.

Atkinson, K. "The Militant Davidic Messiah and Violence against Rome," *Scripta Judaica Cracoviensia* 9 (2011): 7–19.

Aune, David E. "A Note of Jesus' Messianic Consciousness and 11Q Melchizadek," *Evangelical Quarterly* 45, no. 3 (July–September 1973).

Balentine, Samuel E. *The Oxford Encyclopedia of the Bible and Theology.* Oxford: Oxford University Press, 2014.

Ben-Sasson, H. H. *A History of the Jewish People.* Cambridge, MA: Harvard University Press, 1976

Ben-Yehuda, Nachman. *Sacrificing Truth.* New York: Humanity Books, 2002.

Betz, H.D. *The Sermon on the Mount.* Minneapolis, MN: Fortress Press, 1995.

"Book of Enoch." http://www.sacred-texts.com/bib/boe/.

Brown, Raymond. *The Birth of the Messiah.* New York: Doubleday,1977.

———. *The Gospel According to John I-XII.* New York: Doubleday, 1966.

———. *Introduction to the N.T.* New York: Doubleday, 1997.

Brown, Raymond E., Joseph A. Fitzmyer, and Roland E. Murphy, eds. *The Jerome Biblical Commentary.* Englewood Cliffs, NJ: Prentice- Hall, 1968.

———. *The New Jerome Biblical Commentary.* Englewood Cliffs, NJ: Prentice-Hall, 1990.

Capper, Brian. "Public Body, Private Women: The Ideology of Gender and Space and the Exclusion of Women from Public Leadership in the Late First Century Church," in *Theology and the Body*, Robert Hannaford and J'annine Jobling. Leominster: Gracewing, 1999.

Carroll, John T. "Luke's Portrayal of the Pharisees," *Catholic Biblical Quarterly* 50, no. 4 (October 1988): 604–621.

Carter, Warren. " Matthew's Gospel: An Anti-imperial/Imperial Reading," *Currents in Theology and Mission* 34, no. 6 (2007).

Cicero. *De Finibus*, vol. XVII, translation by H. Harris Rackham. Loeb Classical Library, Harvard University Press, second (revised) edition, 1931.

———. "Pro Flacco." http://perseus.uchicago.edu/perseus-cgi/citequery3.pl?dbname =LatinAugust2012&getid=1&query=Cic. Flac. 69.

Clement of Alexandria. "Stromata." http://www.newadvent.org/fathers/0210.htm.

Conzelmann, Hans. *1 Corinthians*. Philadelphia, PA: Fortress Press, 1975.

Crossan, J. *God and Empire*. New York: Harper One, 2007.

———. *In Parables*. San Francisco, CA: Harper & Row, 1985.

———. "The Parables of Jesus," *Interpretation* 56, no. 3 (July 2002): 247–258.

Croy, N. Clayton. "Where the Gospel Text Begins," *Novum Testamentum* 43, no. 2 (2001): 105–127.

Culpepper, R. A. "The Gospel of John and the Jews," *Review and Expositor* 84, no. 2 (1987): 273–288.

Davies, W. D, and D. C. Allison. *A Critical and Exegetical Commentary on the Gospel According to Saint Matthew 1–7*. Edinburgh: T & T Clark, 1988.

"The Damascus Document." http://www.pseudepigrapha.com/pseudepigrapha/ zadokite.html.

Diogenes Laertius. "Lives of Eminent Philosophers." http://www.perseus.tufts.edu/ hopper/text?doc=Perseus%3Atext%3A1999.01.0258%3Abook%3D7%3Achapter %3D1.

Dunn, James D. G. *Christology in the Making*. Philadelphia, PA: Westminster, 1985.

———. *The Evidence for Jesus*. Louisville, KY: Westminster/John Knox, 1986.

———. *The Theology of Paul the Apostle*. Grand Rapids, MI: Eerdmans: 1998.

Dwyer, Timothy. *The Motif of Wonder in the Gospel of Mark*. Sheffield: Sheffield Academic Press, 1996.

Ellis, Peter. *The Genius of John*. Collegeville, MN: Liturgical Press, 1984.

———. *Seven Pauline Letters*. Collegeville, MN: Liturgical Press, 1982.

Finlan, Stephen. *Problems with Atonement: The Origins of, and Controversy about, the Atonement Doctrine*. Collegeville MN: Liturgical Press, 2005.

Fitzmyer, Joseph. *The Gospel According to Luke (XX–XXIV)*. The Anchor Bible. New York: Doubleday, 1986.

Gibson, Jeffrey. *The Temptations of Jesus in Early Christianity*. London: Bloomsbury, 1995.

"The Gospel of Philip." http://gospelofthomas.nazirene.org/philip.htm.

Haddad, Najeeb Turki. "Paul in Context: A Reinterpretation of Paul and Empire," unpublished doctoral dissertation, Loyola Chicago University, 2018.

Häkkinen, Sakari. "Poverty in the First-Century Galilee," *HTS* 72, no.4 (2016).

Hare, D. *The Theme of Jewish Persecution of Christians in St. Matthew*. Cambridge: Cambridge University Press, 1967, 2005.

Hays, Richard B. *1 Corinthians*. Louisville, KY: John Knox, 1997.

Horsley, Richard. *Jesus and the Politics of Roman Palestine*. Columbia: University of South Carolina Press, 2014.

———. "Jesus Movements and the Renewal of Israel," in *A People's History of Christianity*, vol. 1, Dennis Janz. Philadelphia, PA: Fortress Press, 2014.

———. *The Prophet Jesus and the Renewal of Israel*. Grand Rapids, MI: Eerdmans, 2012.

Horsley, Richard, and Tom Thatcher. *John, Jesus, and the Renewal of Israel.* Grand Rapids, MI: Eerdmans, 2013.

Hultgren, Stephen. "The Origin of Paul's Doctrine of the Two Adams in 1 Corinthians 15.45–49," *Journal for the Study of the New Testament* 25, no. 3 (2003): 343–370.

Hurst, L.D. "Did Qumran Expect Two Messiahs?" *Bulletin for Biblical Research* 9 (1999).

Incigneri, Brian J. *The Gospel to the Romans.* Leiden: Brill, 2003

Janssen, L. F. "'Superstitio' and the Persecution of the Christians," *Vigilae Christianae* 33, no. 2 (June 1979): 135–138.

Janz, Dennis. *A People's History of Christianity,* vol. 1. Philadelphia, PA: Fortress Press, 2014.

Josephus, Flavius. "Antiquities of the Jews." http://www.ccel.org/j/josephus/works/JOSEPHUS.HTM.

———. "Wars of the Jews." http://sacred-texts.com/jud/josephus/.

Kahler, Martin. *The So-called Historical Jesus and the Historic Biblical Christ.* Philadelphia: Fortress Press, 1964.

Lewin, Ariel. *The Archaeology of Ancient Judea and Palestine.* Sant Monica, CA: Getty Publications, 2005.

"Lives of the Prophets" in Charlesworth, James. *Old Testament Pseudepigrapha.* Hendrickson Pub; Vol. 2 Edition, 2010.

Marcus, Joel. *Mark 1–8.* Anchor Bible. New York: Doubleday, 2000.

Mason, S. *Josephus, Judea, and Christian Origins.* Ada, MI: Baker Academic 2008.

Matthews, Shelly. *Perfect Martyr.* Oxford: Oxford University Press, 2012.

Meier, John. *Marginal Jew,* vol. 2. New York: Doubleday, 1994.

———. *A Marginal Jew: Rethinking the Historical Jesus, Law, and Love,* vol. 4. New Haven, CT: Yale University Press, 2009.

Miller, Robert. *Helping Jesus Interpret Prophecy.* Eugene, OR: Cascade Books, 2015.

Moloney, Francis J. *The Gospel of John.* Collegeville, MN: Liturgical Press, 1998.

Mott, Stephen. *Biblical Ethics and Social Change.* New York: Oxford University Press, 1982.

Neusner, Jacob. *In Quest of the Historical Pharisees.* Waco, TX: Baylor University Press, 2007.

Newman, Hillel. *Proximity to Power and Jewish Sectarian Groups of the Ancient Period.* Leiden: Brill. 2006.

Oakman. *The Political Aims of Jesus.* Philadelphia, PA: Fortress Press, 2012.

Parke-Taylor, G. H. *Yahweh: The Divine Name in the Bible.* Waterloo, Ontario: Wilfrid Laurier University Press, 1975.

Pawlikowski, John T. *Christ in the Light of the Christian-Jewish Dialog.* Mahwah, NJ: Paulist, 1982.

Perrin, Norman. *The New Testament: An Introduction.* New York: Harcourt Brace Jovanovich, 1974.

Philo. "Allegorical Interpretation." http://www.earlyjewishwritings.com/text/philo/book2.html.

———. "Hypothetica." http://ccat.sas.upenn.edu/rak/courses/999/hypothet.htm.

————. "On the Creation." http://www.earlyjewishwritings.com/text/philo/book1 .html.

Philostratus. "The Life of Apollonius of Tyana." http://www.livius.org /ap- ark/apollonius/life/va_00.html.

Plato. "The Republic." http://classics.mit.edu/Plato/republic.html.

Plutarch. *Moralia*, vol. 4. Loeb Classical Library edition, 1936.

Porter, Stanley E., and Tom Holmén. *Handbook for the Study of the Historical Jesus*. Leiden: Brill, 2011.

"Psalms of Solomon." http://wesley.nnu.edu/sermons-essays-books/noncanonical -literature/noncanonical-literature-ot-pseudepigrapha/the-psalms-of-solomon/.

Rodriguez, R. "The Embarrassing Truth about Jesus" in *Jesus Criteria and the Demise of Authenticity*, Keith Chris and Anthony Le Donne. Edinburgh: T & T Clarke, 2012.

Scheidel, W., and S. Friesen. "The Size of the Economy and the Distribution of Income in the Roman Empire" *Journal of Roman Studies* 99 (November 2009): 61–91.

Scroggs, Robin. *Paul for a New Day*. Philadelphia, PA: Fortress Press, 1977.

Senior, Donald. "The Passion Narrative According to Matthew," Ph.D. diss., Netherlands, Leuven University, 1975.

"Septuagint." http://www.ecmarsh.com/lxx/.

Sharon, Nadav. *Judea Under Roman Domination*. Atlanta, GA: Society of Biblical Literature, 2017.

Tacitus. "The Annals." http://classics.mit.edu/Tacitus/annals.html.

————. "The Histories." http://classics.mit.edu/Tacitus/histories.html.

————. "Life of Cnaeus Julius Agricola." https://sourcebooks.fordham.edu/ancient/ tacitus-agricola.asp.

Terrien, Samuel. *The Elusive Presence*. San Francisco, CA: Harper & Row, 1978.

Udoh, Fabian E. *To Caesar What Is Caesar's: Tribute, Taxes, and Imperial Administration in Early Roman Palestine*. Providence, RI: Brown Judaic Studies, 2020.

Van Eck, Ernest. "The Tenants in the Vineyard (GThom 65/Mark 12:1–12): A Realistic and Social-Scientific Reading," *HTS* 63, no. 3 (2007): 909–936.

Vanhoye, A. *Structure and Theology of the Accounts of the Passion in The Synoptic Gospels*. Collegeville, MN: Liturgical Press, 1967.

Vermes, G. "The Oxford Forum for Qumran Research: Seminar on the Rule of War from Cave 4 (4Q285)," *Journal of Jewish Studies* 43 (Spring 1992).

Yadin, Yigdael. *Masada*. New York: Random House 1987.

York, John. *The Last Shall be First*. London: Bloomsbury 2015.

Zerbe, Gordon. *Non-retaliation in Early Jewish and New Testament Texts*. Sheffield: Sheffield Academic Press, 1993.

Zohar, Noam. "Repentance and Purification," *JBL* 107, no. 4 (1988): 614–615.

Index

About the Author

Robert Imperato, Ph.D., is professor of religion at Saint Leo University. His books include *Early and Medieval Christian Spirituality* (University Press of America, 2003); *Christian Footings* (University Press of America, 2000; revised edition, 2009); and *Merton and Walsh on the Person* (Wipf and Stock, 2014).